SOCIALISTS IN THE RECESSION

Socialists in the Recession

The Search for Solidarity

Giles Radice
and
Lisanne Radice

MACMILLAN
PRESS

First published 1986

Published by
THE MACMILLAN PRESS LTD
Houndmills, Basingstoke, Hampshire RG21 2XS
and London
Companies and representatives
throughout the world

Photoset in 11/12pt Baskerville
by Styleset Limited, Warminster, Wiltshire

Printed in Great Britain by
Anchor Brendon Ltd,
Tiptree, Essex

British Library Cataloguing in Publication Data
Radice, Giles
Socialists in the recession.
1. Socialism—Europe
I. Title   II. Radice, Lisanne
335'.0094   HX239
ISBN 0-333-38845-3 (hardcover)
ISBN 0-333-38846-1 (paperback)

Contents

Preface

The preparation of this book has been greatly assisted by interviews and discussions with politicians, trade unionists, journalists, economists and academics in West Germany, France, Spain, Sweden, Austria and Britain. We are particularly grateful to Kjell-Olof Feldt, Heinz Fischer, Denis Healey, José Maria Maravall, Wolfgang Roth and Axel Quival. We are also grateful to the Policy Studies Institute for support and encouragement. Giles Radice thanks the Ebert Stiftung and the Swedish Institute for their assistance. Lisanne Radice is grateful to the Leverhulme Trust for a research fellowship and to the Anglo-German Foundation for a research grant.

We should like to thank David Blake, Nicholas Butler, David Lipsey, Peter Holmes and Paul Ormerod for their comments on an early draft of Chapter 2. James Plaskitt provided background briefs on West Germany, France and Sweden. Michael Kent helped us with Chapter 6. Geoffrey Norris prepared material for Chapter 10. We are also grateful to the House of Commons Library and to the press cuttings library of the Royal Institute of International Affairs. We are specially indebted to Enid Hutchinson and Gillian Jacomb-Hood who have typed out successive drafts with efficiency and dispatch.

The making of this book has been a joint enterprise. Together we conducted the interviews, carried out the research and planned the book. The final version (prepared by Giles Radice) is based on drafts which were jointly written, discussed and revised. We take joint responsibility for the judgements contained in this book

GILES RADICE
LISANNE RADICE

Introduction

The period of the recession has been a difficult one for European Socialists. Traditionally Socialists have put a high priority on full employment and social spending. Since 1973, after over twenty years of uninterrupted economic expansion, social advance and full employment, there has been a prolonged period of recession and high unemployment. Unemployment in Western Europe is now more than treble the rate in 1973.

Politically, there have been substantial setbacks. In Britain the Labour party has lost the last two elections, in 1983 with its lowest share of the poll since 1918. In West Germany, the Social Democrats (SPD) fell from power in 1982 and lost the subsequent election. In France, the Socialist government was blown off course in 1983 when its relatively modest expansion programme was brought to an abrupt halt by international pressure and, in 1986, was voted out of office. One political commentator has claimed: 'The problem is everywhere the same; there exists no longer either the class base or the moral imperative for a Socialist society. The idea which has gripped the European mind for more than a century has run its course.'[1]

But such a sweeping conclusion ignores Socialist successes. In Austria and Sweden, Socialist administrations have preserved low unemployment and welfare services at a time when right-wing governments have been arguing that it was impossible to do either. In Spain and Greece, Socialists have successfully formed democratic governments in countries in which democracy has only recently been established. Even the setbacks have their silver linings. The French Socialists not only remain the foremost party in France but have also had a better record in bringing down inflation and controlling the rise in unemployment than, for example, Mrs Thatcher's Conservatives; while both the SPD and the British Labour party have staged impressive recoveries.

The time has now come to take a more balanced look at the European Socialist experience since 1973, the year of the first oil shock. The purpose of this book is to examine how the main European Socialist parties have responded to the changed economic climate and how far the main characteristics of the

Socialism of the 1950s and 1960s – a commitment to full employment and economic intervention, to a high level of social spending
and cooperative policies in relationships with other countries –
have been modified by the events of the 1970s and 1980s.

. We seek to draw conclusions both about the differences and
the similarities between parties and also about the general state
of Western European Socialism. We ask whether European
Socialism is a 'fairweather' approach doomed to failure when
the going gets rough or whether there is an enduring strength in
Socialists ideas and policies. The answer is of importance, not
only to committed Socialists, but to all who want to see Western
democracies respond in a more creative and humane way to the
problems of our time.

  The first chapter describes the nature of traditional Democratic Socialism by analysing the experience of the Swedish Social
Democrats, the German Social Democrats and the British
Labour party. The second chapter considers why the economic
climate changed in the 1970s and the impact of the recession.

  The next six chapters examine the political responses and
fortunes of six major European Socialist parties in the 1970s and
1980s. We have chosen the German Social Democrats, the
French Socialist party, the British Labour party, the Spanish
Socialist party, the Swedish Social Democrats and the Austrian
Socialists because they have been among the most popular and
successful of European Socialist parties. Three of the six (the
Spanish, Swedish and Austrian) are in government; in France,
although the Socialists lost the parliamentary elections, there is
still a Socialist President; while all six have been in power during
the last decade. The selection also comprises three parties (the
German Social Democrats, the Austrian Socialists and the
Swedish Social Democrats) which have established supremacy
on the left, two parties (the French and the Spanish Socialists)
which have had to compete with the Communists, and one party
(the British Labour party) which had to surmount a challenge
from the centre.

  The subsequent three chapters compare the record of these
parties in three crucial areas – economic, social and external
affairs. The last chapter draws general conclusions and looks at
prospects for the future.

  Although we are committed Socialists, we have tried to look at
matters as objectively as possible. Where Socialists have made

mistakes, we have said so. Where policies have been found wanting, we have said so. Where changes are needed, we have said so. In the end, despite all the difficulties and problems, we remain optimistic about the future of European Socialism.

Part I
The Background

1 Socialism before the Recession: The Golden Age, 1945–73

The prosperous years of the 1950s and 1960s saw the growth of a new, post-war Social Democracy characterized by a commitment to full employment, Keynesian economic policies, economic and industrial planning, a high level of redistributive social spending, and a partnership with the trade unions. The pattern of European Socialism in those years is best illustrated, not so much by an analysis of philosophy or manifesto, but of how principle was translated into practice. This chapter examines the experience of Socialist parties (the Swedish Social Democrats, the German SPD and the British Labour party) who were in power for substantial periods in the years before the recession.

THE SWEDISH SOCIAL DEMOCRATIC SUCCESS STORY

In the period before 1973 the Swedish Social Democrats were arguably the most successful of all European Socialist parties. They were in power continuously from 1932 and created the most advanced welfare state in Europe, if not the world. In explaining their success, something needs to be said about their origins. Industrialisation came late and rapidly to Sweden, coinciding with the formation in 1889 of the Swedish Social Democrats. The pace and timing of the Swedish industrialisation had two consequences: firstly, the unions (organised on an industrial basis) and the party grew up 'two branches of the same tree'[1] and worked extremely closely together. Secondly, the Social Democrats, with a thin trade union base, became the natural party not just for most industrial workers but for the overwhelming majority of them.

The relatively late achievement of universal suffrage was also a factor in the rise of the Social Democrats. At the end of the last century a high level of literacy and a considerable degree of

7

freedom of expression and popular organisation coexisted with a situation in which only a quarter of male adults had the right to vote and there was no parliamentary control of the executive. The Social Democrats joined the Liberals in the battle for the vote – a battle which was not won until the end of the First World War. The party was not only able to draw credit from its contribution to the struggle but also to benefit electorally from the wider franchise.

A third factor in the rise of the Social Democrats to power was the division among the so-called 'bourgeois' parties. The presence of a strong independent peasantry was a barrier in the way of the kind of alliance between the landed and urban interests which formed the basis for the emergence of a strong Conservative party in Britain. In fact, an Agrarian party (now the Centre party) was formed in 1913. In addition, the Swedish Liberal party, while not a serious rival to the Social Democrats for the working-class vote, had a sufficient difference in attitude, policy and type of support to maintain a separate identity from the Swedish Conservatives. Thus in the crucial period during which the Social Democrats emerged as the dominant party in Swedish politics the non-Socialist parties were divided.

Swedish conditions also shaped the approach of the Swedish Social Democrats. In its insistence on the eventual abolition of private property and public ownership of all the means of production, the 1897 programme was Marxist, but already there was a reference to socialisation 'by degrees' and a clear recognition of the possibilities which democracy could open up for the working classes. Until the end of the First World War the achievement of political democracy was the main aim of the party, so much so that 'through parliamentary activity in the increased democratic state, democracy itself came to be considered not only as a means but a fundamental principle'.[2] As a consequence of its close links with the trade unions, it also gave priority to industrial issues such as unemployment insurance, the expansion of public works and the eight-hour day.

During the 1920s, the Social Democrats, though the biggest party, could never achieve an overall majority and formed three short-lived minority governments under Branting. It was not until the 1930s that the party was able to achieve effective power, and the price of power was, first, agreement, and in 1936, coalition with the Agrarian party. It is, in part, this background of political compromise which has led many commentators to see the Social Democrats as a pragmatic, social reformist party par excellence.[3] A more convincing explanation is that, though they have always given a high priority to building a progressive consensus and have been consistently and courageously prepared to adapt means and policies to changing conditions, they have also retained a deep respect for the commitment to Socialist objectives – equality, freedom, security, solidarity and the need to secure social control over the economy. Their highly effective response to the great depression of the 1930s illustrates both this commitment to Socialist objectives and a willingness to adopt unorthodox policies to achieve them.

STOCKHOLM KEYNESIANISM

In 1932, four years before the publication of Keynes' *General Theory*, a Swedish Social Democratic government introduced a strongly counter-cyclical spending programme. It was highly successful. Unemployment was reduced from 164 000 in 1933 to 18 000 by 1937.

In the face of the economic crisis, the Swedish Social Democrats, like the British Labour party in 1929–31, could have adopted conservative economic policies or, like the German Socialists in 1930, awaited impotently the disintegration of the capitalist system. Instead, a group within the party, led by Ernst Wigförss, a leading theoretician, and advised by the Stockholm School of Economists, developed a new strategy which was designed to boost consumption, investment and employment by public works and deficit government spending. When asked in the Swedish Parliament how such a policy could create enough jobs, Wigförss replied that

> If I want to start jobs for 100 persons it is not necessary that I put all of the 100 to work. It is so fortunate in this world that if I can give a job to an unemployed tailor, then he can afford to get a new pair of shoes and in this way an unemployed shoemaker will get work. . . .The crisis is characterised. . .by something which is called the vicious circle and which means that first the income of some persons is lowered and this means that those persons who used to supply their goods can

now no longer sell their goods and. . .become unemployed. . . .
The crisis feeds itself. . .but it is also so when the recovery
starts.[4]

This new economic policy not only increased production and
greatly reduced unemployment. It also helped to lay the basis for
the political dominance which the Social Democrats were to
enjoy over the next forty-four years.

BUILDING THE 'PEOPLE'S HOME'

From the 1930s to the mid-1960s, Swedish Social Democrat
governments developed the most advanced welfare state in the
world, making Per Albin Hanson's visionary concept of Sweden
as a 'People's Home' a reality. This remarkable welfare achievement was based on a growing economy, a high level of redistributive public spending and considerable degree of social
consensus.

The system established by the Swedish Social Democrats has
been described as 'the politics of virtuous circles'.[5] It had three
main ingredients. One was an 'historic compromise' with
capital. In 1938 Wigförss made a famous speech to the Gothen-
burg Bourse Society in which he argued that both the working-
class movement and the private capitalists should recognise that
neither could hope to suppress each other and that they should
therefore cooperate to achieve their common interest – increased
efficiency in production. After the war (in which the Swedes
remained neutral), the Erlander governments developed this
strategy of compromise more fully in the so-called 'Harpsund
democracy'. Industry would remain in private hands so long as it
continued to expand and provide the resources required to
ensure social welfare for all.

It should be noted that the Social Democrats did not see this
agreement as an abandonment of their Socialist objectives. On
the contrary, they believed that, in postwar political and
economic conditions, greater equality and welfare could only be
achieved through such an agreement. The Social Democrats were
prepared to accept that only about 10 per cent of industry would
be publicly owned and that the remainder would be increasingly
concentrated in fewer and fewer hands (by 1976 the Swedish

TUC estimated that only 100 people directed the main industrial decisions). But in return, they were able to ensure that the Swedish economy grew at an average of four per cent a year throughout the 1950s and 1960s and that Swedish per capita income became one of the highest in the world.

What is even more important, the Social democrats used the wealth which growth created to finance the most extensive social services in the world, including unemployment insurance, pensions, public health and medical care, child and housing allowances, as well as good quality housing and a comprehensive educational system. In a comparative welfare study in 1974 of the twenty-five OECD countries (based on key indicators including the level of government revenue as a percentage of GDP, educational spending, infant mortality rates and GDP per capita) Sweden came comfortably top.[6] The less well off in Sweden received better medical care, higher pensions and enjoyed access to a wider range of public services and public benefits than in almost any other society, while the living standards of the broad mass of industrial workers were amongst the highest in the world.

The success of Social Democratic governments in improving the living standards of the industrial workers was linked to the second ingredient in 'the politics of virtuous circles' – the Social Democratic government's close collaboration with trade unions. In return for guarantees of full employment, an equitable share of national wealth, and increased welfare, the trade unions were prepared to minimise industrial conflict, operate a highly effective, (if unofficial and entirely voluntary) incomes policy, and work to enhance productivity. From the mid-1930s onwards, Sweden, which until then had had one of the highest rates of industrial disputes, earned a well-merited reputation for industrial harmony. The symbol of this new state of affairs was the 1938 Saltsjöbaden agreement between the Swedish Trade Union Confederation (LO) and the Central Employers Organisation which was designed to regulate collective bargaining and industrial relations, so that disputes, particularly in the public services, could be settled 'without resort to open conflict'. One of the motives behind this agreement was the desire to avoid state intervention. But the decisive factor for the trade unions was the existence of a Social Democratic government able to deliver full employment and increased welfare.

After the war, the Swedish trade unions rapidly understood that economic growth and full employment would be endangered if they used their new bargaining power to the full. In 1951 the LO (the Swedish TUC) set up a Wage Policy Council whose function was to prepare guidelines for trade union bargaining in the light not only of the results of previous settlements but also of economic trends and prospects. By the end of the 1950s, LO central agreements determined the pattern for the whole economy. Despite wage drift, it is significant that increases in money earnings were usually in line with increases in productivity 'so that the thesis which has often been advanced that the LO has generated cost increases which put the competitives of Swedish industry at risk is difficult to sustain'.[7]

Swedish trade unions were persuaded that it was in their interests to help improve productivity, particularly in Sweden's vital export industries. LO policy took two forms. Firstly, they were prepared to use the strength of central bargaining to push up the wages of the low paid, even if that meant pushing the less productive firms out of business. But, secondly, if that occurred, or if regional unemployment 'blackspots' developed, then they collaborated in the development of an 'active manpower policy'. According to the Rehn–Meidner strategy (after its LO authors) the state would intervene selectively in the labour market in support of training, effective employment creation and placement, and location of industry and investment in order to provide jobs for the unemployed and to shift labour from the inefficient to the efficient firms and industries. The LO 'active manpower policy' was accepted by Social Democratic governments and became a central part of their economic strategy. By 1973 the expenditure of the National Labour Movement Board amounted to 8 per cent of total government expenditure. One indication of the success of the manpower policy was that at the time of the first oil shock the unemployment rate was only 2 per cent.

The third ingredient in the politics of virtuous circles was the continuing political dominance of the Swedish Social Democrats. A high degree of industrial and social consensus led to economic growth, rising living standards and expanding welfare. The Social Democrats' reward was electoral victory: until the 1970s their share of the vote never fell below 45 per cent and in 1968 they actually won over 50 per cent. It is significant that, though they also received support from other groups, particularly white-collar workers, their proportion of the industrial working-class vote was the highest of any party in Western Europe. By their success in government, built in part on their close relationship with the unions and their historic compromise with capital, they created the electoral support for continued government and, more enduringly, for the permeation of Swedish society by the Democratic Socialist values of social justice, welfare and solidarity, so that, even when they lost power, their political opponents were unable to dismantle the welfare state which the Social Democrats created.

THE SPD: THE CLASSIC REVISIONIST PARTY

The SPD was also successful, though their period in government was confined to the seven years immediately before the first oil shock. Under its fiery leader, Kurt Schumacher, the SPD had fully expected to dominate the politics of postwar Western Germany. It was true that in the Weimar Republic the SPD, imprisoned by its Marxist ideology, had totally failed to provide the answer to the slump. It had also failed to put up an effective resistance to Hitler. But they were the oldest and most respected Socialist party in Europe and their leaders had either been in Nazi concentration camps or in exile, so their democratic credentials were impeccable. However it was the Christian Democrats which, under the septuagenarian ex-mayor of Cologne, Konrad Adenauer, won three successive elections – in 1949, 1953 and 1957.

Apart from Adenauer's immense political skill and undoubted popularity with many West Germans, there were four main reasons why the Social Democrats kept losing elections. The first was that, with the postwar division of Germany, they lost areas of working-class support in the East, while the Christian Democrats were able to appeal to Catholic workers in the West.

Secondly, under Schumacher's direction, the SPD opposed plans to integrate West Germany into Western Europe on the grounds that this would legitimise the de facto division of Germany and would prevent external unification. But the majority of West Germany saw initiatives such as Marshall Aid, the European Coal and Steel Commission, the European

Defence Community and West German membership of NATO as providing the necessary framework for protecting their security and ensuring a rising standard of living.

Thirdly, with East Germany under the control of a hardline Communist regime, the Social Democrats found their old Marxist antecedents a decided electoral handicap. Schumacher tried to shift the emphasis away from Marxism. He commented: 'It is no matter whether someone becomes a Social Democrat through the methods of Marxist analysis, for philosophical or ethical reasons, or out of the spirit of the sermon on the Mount.' He also argued that 'Socialism is no longer the affair of the working class in the old sense of the world. It is the programme for workers, farmers, artisans, tradesmen and the intellectual professions.' Even so, the formal position of the SPD remained Marxist, which enabled the CDU to campaign in the 1953 election on the misleading but highly effective slogan: 'All Marxist roads lead to Moscow – vote CDU.'

The fourth and perhaps greatest difficulty for the Social Democrats was the amazingly swift recovery of the West German economy. The combination of an undervalued mark, a plentiful labour supply (two and half million Germans left East for West Germany between 1949 and 1961), good industrial relations, a high level of investment, and the psychological as well as economic boost provided by the Marshall Plan, quickly produced sustained export-led growth. Between 1950 and 1960, the expansion of West German output was the fastest in Europe and, at the 1957 elections, the CDU could with justice point to their achievement of full employment and a rapidly increasing standard of living for most West Germans. Although inequalities actually increased during the 1950s (partly because the share of the national income going to wages fell), there was little Erich Ollenhauer, Schumacher's lack-lustre successor, could do to counter the CDU's 'You've never had it so good' claims. In 1957 the SPD may have marginally increased its share (from 28 per cent to 31 per cent) but the Christian Democrats actually won over 50 per cent of votes cast – an impressive electoral performance by any standards.

It was against the background of electoral defeat that the SPD adopted, by an overwhelming majority, a new party programme at a special party conference at Bad Godesburg in 1959. The Bad Godesburg programme represented a signal to the West German electorate that it had broken decisively with its Marxist past and that it was attempting to build a progressive majority which would give the SPD power for the first time in the Federal Republic.

'BAD GODESBURG' AND AFTER

The new Socialism of Bad Godesburg was ethical in character and firmly democratic in its methods. It boldly stated that 'Freedom, justice and solidarity which are everyone's obligation towards his neighbour and spring from our common humility are the fundamental values of Socialism' and that Socialism 'is a continuous task of fighting for freedom and justice, of preserving them, and of proving itself in them'. It also underlined its opposition to dictatorship, whether of right or of left, and reaffirmed that Socialism 'can only be put into practice through democracy; democracy achieves fulfilment through Socialism'. The programme's main author, Willi Eichler, called it 'an ethical revolution'.

In contrast to previous SPD programmes, the Bad Godesburg programme did not support total public ownership of all the means of production, distribution and exchange. Instead, it accepted the idea of private ownership 'provided this does not hinder the establishment of a just social order'. This proviso was extremely important. It is not true (as Dr David Owen, leader of the British Social Democrat party, has eroneously argued)[8] that Bad Godesburg represented an unconditional acceptance of the market economy. The programme specifically stated that 'whenever large enterprises predominate there is no free competition', and warned that, 'through their power, which is enhanced even more by cartels and associations, the leading men of big business are gaining an influence in the state and position which is not reconcilable with democratic principles.' It concluded that when 'a healthy ordering of economic power or relationships cannot be guaranteed by other means, public ownership is purposeful and necessary.' It also embraced Keynesian policies and a major role for the state in economic and industrial planning. The formula adopted at Bad Godesburg was 'competition as far as possible, planning as far as necessary'.[9]

The other main emphasis of Bad Godesburg was on the need

to create a 'social state'. Strongly influenced by the SPD, the 1949 'Basic Law' had laid down that the Federal Republic should seek to establish an equitable social and economic order. The Bad Godesburg programme argued that 'the social function of the state is to provide social security for its citizens. . .the state becomes a truly civilised state through the fusion of the democratic idea with the ideas of social security and the rule of law.' It outlined an ambitious plan of social reforms, including extensions of social security and health protection, expansion of the housing programme, reduction in working hours, more co-determination, opening up education to provide for future life chances and redistribution of income and wealth.

Bad Godesburg was certainly the programme of a party which was concerned to turn its back on Marxism to widen its electoral appeal. But those who argue that it also represented an abandonment of Socialist principles and goals have not only to take into account the commitment to planning and redistributive social spending but also the comment of Willy Brandt, SPD Chairman for thirty years and highly respected guardian of the party's ideological direction. In 1979, he said that "it has been asserted that the Godesburg programme implies "a renunciation of Socialism" but those who take this view are badly mistaken'.[10]

It took ten more years after Bad Godesburg before Brandt became the first SPD Chancellor in the Federal Republic. A key landmark in the rise of the SPD was the decision to join a 'grand coalition' with the Christian Democrats in 1966. Although the CDU had won more votes than the SPD in the 1965 elections, and was able to form a coalition with the FDP, the economy deteriorated during 1966 and the unemployment rose. The recession (a small one by the standards of the 1970s) was purely domestic and had been engineered by the independent Bundesbank, which was more concerned by the rate of inflation than by the need to maintain full employment. The Christian Democrats, deeply disturbed by unemployment and deserted by their junior coalition partner, turned to the Social Democrats. A big coalition was formed with the CDU's nominee, Kurt Georg Kiesinger, as Chancellor and Willy Brandt as Vice-Chancellor and Foreign Minister.

Obviously, going into coalition with their main political rivals was a risk. But there were considerable advantages. The SPD's

Keynesian approach was officially adopted by the coalition. By the stabilisation laws of 1967 the Federal Government for the first time accepted responsibility for managing the economy. Under the coalition, the first tentative approaches towards detente with Germany's eastern neighbours were also taken. Above all, the grand coalition brought the SPD in from the cold. Wehner, the main architect of the grand coalition strategy, was understandably fearful that, unless West Germans actually saw the SPD in government, it would come to be considered as a party of permanent opposition. As Brandt wrote later,[11] the grand coalition gave the SPD a chance to prove itself in power – a chance which they took with both hands.

THE SPD IN POWER

The SPD's strategy was justified by the 1969 election result when, for the first time, the SPD won over 40 per cent of the vote and, together with the FDP, was able to form a new SPD-led coalition. Willy Brandt became Federal Chancellor. Brandt who came from the poorest section of the North German working class, spent the period of Nazi rule in Scandinavian exile and, at the end of the war, actually became a Norwegian citizen. However, in 1946 he went to Berlin and in 1957 was elected Mayor of West Berlin. Twice defeated as the SPD's candidate for Chancellor, he was fully entitled to claim on his election that now Hitler had finally lost the war. Speaking to foreign journalists, he said, 'I see myself as the Chancellor of a liberated not a defeated, Germany.'[12] Brandt's Chancellorship represents the high-water mark of postwar German Social democracy.

In foreign affairs, the Brandt Government is justly celebrated for its *Ost politik*. In government, the SPD was determined to achieve three things–improved relations with the Soviet Union, normal relations with East European states and a modus vivendi between the two parts of Germany. For Brandt, *Ost politik* represented not only an acceptance of the post-war European settlement and a desire to secure a detente in Eastern Europe, but was also an attempt to create a climate in which peaceful change might eventually become possible

A series of treaties was signed with West Germany's eastern neighbours and with the Soviet Union, Poland and the GDR. At the same time there was an agreement on Berlin between the Western allies and the Soviet Union. A key element of the new settlement was the acceptance by West Germany of the Oder/ Neisse line as the frontier between East Germany and Poland, which speedily led to better relations, symbolised by Brandt's historic gesture of kneeling before the Ghetto memorial in Warsaw. The basic treaty between the two Germanys was more difficult to negotiate and was not signed until December 1972. It formally recognised the existence of the two countries and established official relations between them. Working closely with his Western allies, Brandt had skilfully created the conditions for a better understanding in Central and Eastern Europe.

Brandt was not only a 'foreign policy' Chancellor. He was also a *Kunzler der inneren Reformen* (Chancellor of domestic reform). Under Brandt, the growth rate continued to be one of the highest in Europe, while unemployment never rose above two per cent. This successful stewardship of the economy was based on a con- tinuation of Keynesian demand management, a more active industrial and labour market policy and an unofficial but highly effective understanding with the trade unions on the growth of incomes.

The coalition's economic success provided a strong base for the government's social reforms. These included the introduc- tion of voluntary retirement at 63, the extension of pension rights, the provision of sick pay for industrial workers, an expanded health insurance scheme and support for low income tenants and householders. Family allowances, pensions, injury and sickness benefits were all increased substantially, while war victims' pensions were linked to wage increases. The Govern- ment also widened educational opportunities. Spending on education and research rose by nearly 300 per cent, between 1970 and 1974. The school leaving age was raised to 16. Grants were provided to encourage pupils from lower income groups to stay on at school. Grants were also made available for those going into any kind of higher or further education, fees were abolished and the number of higher education institutions were substan- tially increased. However, because education was primarily a regional responsibility, the Government was unable to introduce reform of secondary education on comprehensive lines. Even so, Helmut Becker, an authoritative commentator on German education, has estimated that, as a consequence of the coalition's educational reforms, there was greater achievement at all levels and that the chances of a 20-year-old working-class child born in 1958 reaching a university or college was approximately six times greater than it was for a similar child born in 1948.[13]

Brandt was a committed democrat who had suffered for his beliefs and was convinced of the need for a dialogue with an increasingly sophisticated West German electorate, particularly young people. But it was not just a matter of style. He also intended to introduce democratic reforms 'to transform more and more people into responsible decision-makers'.[14] In 1972 a new Factory Management law was passed extending co-determination at the factory level. But the FDP vetoed the SPD plan to extend parity co-determination at work level to all industries; this change was not introduced until 1976.

Judged both from the point of view of specific reforms in social and educational policy and from the overall increases in public spending (from 37.6 per cent of GDP in 1969 to 40.5 per cent in 1973), the Brandt Government was undoutedly a successful reforming administration. Its popularity was demonstrated by the results of the 1972 Bundestag elections when, for the first time in the Federal Republic, the SPD became the biggest single party, receiving strong support from trade unions, the young and women.

However in the months following the election, the reelected coalition ran into trouble. In May 1973 the Government introduced tough restrictive measures to curb inflation and, at the end of 1973, also had to face the first oil shock. In addition, the SPD suffered from internal conflicts between its youth wing and the leadership. There were heavy losses in the local elections. Early in 1974 Brandt was forced to resign, when one of his closest aides was arrested as a spy, and he was succeeded as Chancellor by Helmut Schmidt.

BRITISH LABOUR GOVERNMENTS 1964–70: A MISSED OPPORTUNITY

In the period before the recession, the British Labour party was less successful than either the Swedish Social Democrats or the SPD. Despite the considerable achievements of the Wilson Government in 1964–70, it failed to establish the Labour Party as the predominant force in British politics. It was a missed opportunity.

The foundations of postwar British society had been laid by the Attlee Government on 1945–51. Profiting from the desire for change and from the reputation which Labour leaders had gained as ministers in the wartime coalition, Labour had been elected in 1945 with a huge majority. The Attlee administration used Keynesian measures to establish full employment, took basic industries into public ownership, introduced the National Health Service and a comprehensive system of social security, brought about a fairer division of income through redistributive taxation and benefits, and gave independence to India, Pakistan, Burma and Ceylon. Its record as a reforming government was extremely impressive.

However, as in Western Germany, it was a revived Conservative party which dominated the politics of the 1950s. By 1951 the old Labour leadership was exhausted, while there was fierce internal dissension as to the future direction of the party. Labour lost three successive elections in 1951, 1955 and 1959, each time by a bigger margin. Following the 1959 defeat, the Labour Party leader, Hugh Gaitskell, made an attempt to do a British 'Bad Godesburg' by getting Clause IV of the Labour party constitution amended. However, partly for reasons of sentiment, partly because Clause IV was not, in any case, a purely Marxist statement,[15] and partly because of the sheer lack of preparation, he was decisively defeated.[16] Without tampering with the party's consititution, his successor, Harold Wilson, was far more successful in giving Labour an approach which would appeal to affluent working-class and professional middle-class voters.

The Labour party fought the 1964 election as the party capable of expanding the economy and modernising Britain by opening up British society to all ranks. In the stirring rhetoric of Harold Wilson, Labour promised to:

> replace the closed, exclusive society by an open society in which all have an opportunity to work and serve, in which brains will take precedence over blue blood, and craftsmanship will be more important than caste. Labour wants to streamline our institutions, modernise methods of government, bring the entire nation into a working partnership with the state.[17]

Labour committed itself to 'change the face and future of Britain' by a combination of economic and industrial planning, a partnership with the trade unions on incomes, educational reform, better housing and a fairer, more generous social security system. Labour won the 1964 election narrowly but was confirmed in power by a substantial majority in 1966.

Labour's Record

How far did Labour live up to its promise? In some respects, its performance was praiseworthy.[18] First, there was a substantial increase in public spending between 1964 and 1969 – the last full year of Labour government – from 33.9 per cent to 41.5 per cent of GDP. Education, health and social security benefits all increased their share of the national product; only defence suffered a cut. Its record on public spending was a clear indication of the government's priorities.

Secondly, as a consequence of government policy, the distribution of income became more equal. Although there has been controversy over the issue, the most convincing evidence suggests that (mainly as a result of big increases in cash benefits) pensioners, large families and the unemployed gained more in terms of real disposable income than the rest of the population. In addition, there was also a substantial increase in benefits in kind, notably in education and health. One authority concluded:

> It would appear then, that there was an improvement in the distribution of income, both vertical and horizontal under the Labour Government . . . . To have promoted a measurable improvement in the distribution of income against the background of the deplorably slow rate of growth . . . was one of the Labour Government's main achievements.[19]

Thirdly, there was an improvement in educational opportunities. Expenditure on education rose from 4.8 per cent of GNP in 1964 to 6.1 per cent in 1970 – a larger share than that of defence spending. Circular 10/65 gave a decisive impetus to comprehensive secondary education. There was a steady reduction in pupil–teacher ratios. And there was a major expansion of higher education, with a distinct bias towards the non-university sector. As a result of this effort, it is fair to say that all classes in the community enjoyed more education in 1970 than before, while opportunities for working-class children improved significantly.

Fourthly, there were important reforms in the area of personal liberties. The Government presided over an impressive list of radical social and penal legislation, covering abortion, capital punishment, homosexuality, divorce law, theatre censorship and complaints against the bureaucracy.

In external affairs, the Government's record was more open to criticism. There was the ineffective handling of the admittedly intractable issue of Rhodesia. There was the support for American intervention in Vietnam. And it was only because of financial pressure that the Government was persuaded to abandon its 'East of Suez' role, with the Prime Minister himself being a 'late convert'. The fact remains that it was under the 1964–70 Labour Government that Britain finally discarded its old worldwide role and began to come to terms with its status as a medium-size European power.

THE FAILURE TO ACHIEVE GROWTH

The central failure of the Wilson Government was economic – and for this failure Wilson himself must carry much of the blame. Admittedly, the growth in domestic output of 2.3% a year between 1964 and 1970 looks better in retrospect than it did at the time. But the trend has to be set against the performance in the same period of Britain's main industrial rivals and against the previous six years of Conservative government; in both cases the comparison is to Labour's disadvantage.

Growth was vital to the Wilson Government's plans. If output had been greater, there would have been more for public spending. More would have been available for consumption. Sustained growth would also have strengthened the economy at a time when the opportunities for British industry in world markets were potentially extremely promising. Last but not least, it would have substantially improved Labour's electoral prospects.

The explanation of British Labour's lack of success in achieving a higher level of growth lies not in a failure to take more industries or companies under public control (though there may have been arguments for that), or to set up the appropriate planning machinery (though the National Plan was very much a first attempt at national planning), but in the decision by the Labour Government, and particularly by its Prime Minister, to maintain sterling at the existing exchange rate. It would be idle to pretend that devaluation in October 1964 or at the latest in July 1966 would have solved all Britain's economic and industrial problems. What it would have done was to stimulate the demand for British exports and help solve the balance of payments problem. Given that world trade was expanding so fast, it might also have led, as in Western Germany, to a sustained period of export-led growth. It is certain that squeezing the economy, as had happened in July 1965 and, to a much greater extent, in July 1966, to preserve the exchange rate, sacrificed growth to prop up the unsustainable.

In its attempt to uphold the value of sterling, the Labour Government also used up its credit with the trade unions. The 1964 Government was able to gain the support of the trade unions for a prices and incomes policy because, it argued, it would help create the conditions for growth. In practice, however, it was used to help maintain the exchange rate. When the Government finally devalued in November 1967 and needed a further period of restraint to preserve the gains of devaluation, resentment had already began to build up, particularly at grass roots level. In 1968, the Government made matters worse by attempting to introduce industrial relations legislation in the face of trade union hostility.

At the 1970 election, the Government, despite its undoubted social and educational achievements and its eventual success, after the waste of its first three years, in combining a respectable degree of growth with a healthy balance of payments, was turned out of office. Many working-class supporters were unimpressed both by the squeeze on consumption in 1968 and 1969 and by a complacent Labour campaign and stayed at home. Thus, at a time of maximum opportunity and when the rewards for electoral success would have been very great, Labour sadly failed to become the dominant force in British politics.

CONCLUSION: THE PATTERN OF PRE-1973 SOCIALISM

From this summary, the pattern of Socialism before the recession becomes clear: Keynesian economic policies to maintain activity and employment, an element of economic and industrial planning and intervention, a high level of social spending, an emphasis on educational reform, and a partnership with trade unions, were common to the approach of the three parties whose experiences we have discussed.

Of course, there were differences. The British Labour Government of 1964–70, with its National Plan, its nationalisation of the steel industry, its establishment of an Industrial Re-organisation Corporation and its ambitious regional policies, was more directly interventionist in the industrial sphere than either the Swedish Social Democrats or the Brandt administration in West Germany. This was partly because the British Labour tradition was more interventionist (after all, the 1945–51 Labour Government had nationalised the basic utilities) and partly because British industry was more inefficient than Swedish and certainly West German industry. Even so, the Swedes put considerable resources and effort into their interventionist labour market policies (including training, employment creation and location of industry and investment), while the SPD introduced a more active regional and industrial policy.

But the similarities were far more striking than the differences. In particular, all three Socialist governments deliberately increased social spending as part of their plans to ensure that the standard of living of the less well off – the pensioners, the large families, the unemployed, the sick, the handicapped – was improved. All three embarked on strategies to widen educational opportunities and all three believed in a close partnership with their respective trade union movement.

Paradoxically, the British Labour Government, which had the closest organic ties with trade unions (in Sweden, the link is only at local party level, while in West Germany there is no formal relationship at all), had the most difficulty in preserving the partnership. This was in part due to errors of judgment by the government ministers (as we have seen) and in part due to the more decentralised and competitive nature of the British trade unions. But the idea of some kind of compact with the trade unions to exercise an element of restraint on increases in incomes in order to create the conditions for stable growth, rising standards of living and generous welfare programmes was central to the Socialist experience before 1973.

Despite the different geographical and historial circumstances, there were also some similarities in their approach to external relations. Sweden, of course, had a tradition of neutrality, while both Britain and West Germany were members of NATO. But all three governments took, on the whole, a non-aggressive, cooperative attitude to foreign policy. Willy Brandt was given the Nobel Peace Prize for his efforts towards detente in Eastern Europe, while Harold Wilson, though in many ways much more conservative in foreign policy, sought to act as mediator in Vietnam and successfully cut defence spending. All three governments put a high priority on aid to Third World countries. Finally, all three governments supported the principle of free trade, at least in industrial goods, mainly because they believed that the expansion of international trade since the war had benefited their economies and their profits.

What of their achievements? First, all three governments maintained full employment. The Swedish Social Democrat record was far the most impressive in that not only was it the first government to put what later come to be called Keynesian economics into practice, but maintained full employment throughout its period in office. However, the SPD first came to office in 1966 when it joined the grand coalition on the condition counter-cyclical policies were applied to overcome growing unemployment in West Germany; and it successfully preserved full employment, at least until the recession. Under the Wilson administration, unemployment was a little higher at 2.3 per cent but it should be noted that its record was considerably better than the pre-recession level of its Conservative successor. Of course, full employment was not exclusively a Socialist achievement. In other European countries, other governments also obtained and then preserved full employment. But this was, at least in part, because in the overwhelming majority of cases they too pursued Keynesian policies (see chapter 2).

With respect to growth of output, rates in both Sweden and Western Germany under Socialist governments were consistently impressive, though, as we have seen, the record of the Wilson administration was less good. Once again, it is certainly the case that non-Socialist governments (again, in part because of their adoption of Keynesian policies) presided over economies with high growth rates. The crucial difference is the much greater emphasis that Socialist governments gave to ensuring that, mainly through increases in social spending and benefits but also through re-distributive taxation, the fruits of growth were more fairly shared. It should also be noted that, in the case of Sweden and West Germany, a dynamic policy of public spending was compatible with a high rate of growth in output.

It is necessary, however, to mention two criticisms of the Socialist record in the years before the recession. Right-wing monetarists have argued that the increases in public spending threatened growth because it led to inflation, while left-wing critics believed that Socialist governments did not have sufficient impact on social inequalities and had left the old power structure virtually intact.

The monetarist case is dealt with more fully in the next chapter. It should, however, be said that there is little evidence that increases in the share of the national product going to public spending in the 1960s and the early 1970s led to increases in inflation or that the level of inflation grew faster in West Germany, Britain and Sweden than in comparable countries. Though all three governments were committed to Keynesian strategies, they pursued fiscally responsible policies. Growth in public spending was financed out of growth in national output and by increases in rates of taxation. Nor is there any evidence that the government increases in public spending was at the expense of investment in industry. Of course, conservatives often consider that any increase in the size of state activities is per se bad. But that is a view that is more an ideological belief than a tenable economic hypothesis.

The left-wing case is more compelling. Anthony Crosland had contended that 'Socialism was about equality' but there was no denying that, despite Socialist successes, there remained large differences in income and wealth, even in Sweden where the Social Democrats had been in power for many years. The achievements of the Swedish Social Democrats had been considerable. According to one authority, they had succeeded in alleviating 'the condition of the unfortunate' and creating 'a wide middle structure, including the mass of the industrial working class'.[20] But in the early 1970s, official commissions (set up through party pressure) revealed that there remained a significant minority of the very rich and that some groups, particularly the disabled, were still in poverty. Even so, the egalitarian transformation of Sweden under the Social democrats (though to a lesser extent in West Germany under the SPD and Britain under Labour) had been marked.

With respect to the power structures, there is little doubt that educational reforms (again particularly in Sweden but also in Britain and West Germany) opened up new opportunities for children from working-class backgrounds.[21] It is also the case that in all three countries, strong trade union movements, with their power increased by full employment and sympathetic governments, were able to exercise significant influence both within industry and at a national level. Furthermore in Sweden, the prolonged political dominance of the Social Democrats had a profound impact on the power and value structures of society. It was no exaggeration to say that because of the many years of Social Democrat government, the dominant image of society was Social Democratic.[22] The impact of the German SPD and the British Labour party on their respective countries was less strong, in part because of the existence of powerful right-wing parties. Even so, in the period between 1960 and 1973, the ideas of welfare, redistribution and reform were also extremely influential in West Germany and Britain.

2 The Climate Changes: The Impact of Recession

The economic background to the development of postwar European Socalism was one of unprecedented expansion. In the twenty years between 1953 and 1973, the annual growth rate in Western Europe was 4.8 per cent, nearly double that of the period from 1922 to 1937 and over double that of the period from 1870 to 1913. Investment levels were also higher, while for the first time in European history there was a sustained period of full employment. All Western European countries, including even the United Kingdom with its sluggish economy, shared in this advance.

But in the early 1970s the climate changed dramatically. In 1975, for the first time since the war, Europe's GDP actually fell by nearly one per cent. Despite a subsequent recovery, the growth and investment rates during the 1970s were much lower than in the 1950s and 1960s, while unemployment rose sharply. In 1979–80, there was a further more serious setback. Recession was much more prolonged, unemployment climbed still higher and growth did not pick up until the end of 1982, and even then at a rate below that of the 70s.

This chapter considers briefly the causes of Western Europe's period of expansion in 1950s and 1960s, what went wrong in the early 1970s, examines the response to the two oil shocks, and explores some of the features of the economic environment of the late 1980s.

THE CAUSES OF GROWTH

A number of reasons have been suggested to explain the accelerated European expansion of the 1950s and 1960s. Some commentators have pointed to predominantly supply-side factors, such as the availability of labour, raw materials and cheap technology.[1]

It is certainly the case that there was an abundant supply of agricultural and Southern European workers for the factories of postwar Western Europe. The extent of the shift from the land is demonstrated by the huge decline in agricultural employment from 30 per cent in 1950 to 10 per cent in 1980. Western Europe was also able to draw freely on relatively cheap raw materials from the rest of the world. In addition, there was a wide range of American technical inventions available for development by European firms and industries. However, it is unlikely that these supply-side factors can provide a sufficient explanation for this period of 'super growth', especially as they had also been present to a considerable degree in earlier periods.

A more convincing and complete explanation emphasises the part played by postwar economic policies.[2] At the international level, the establishment under American leadership of a new economic order, based on fixed exchange rates and free trade, greatly assisted reconstruction in the 1940s and growth in the 1950s and 1960s.

The enlighted attitude of the United States was undoubtedly a major factor in Western European recovery. Instead of insisting on the repayment of war debts (as after the First World War), the United States provided abundant long-term finance for reconstruction in the form of Marshall Aid. Western European countries also benefited greatly from being able to export freely and (in some cases) at undervalued rates of exchange to North American markets, despite a growing and prolonged United States balance of payments deficit. Intra-European trade was also stimulated by the formation of the European Economic Community. The part played by trade in West European economies is indicated by the fact that between 1950 and 1973 both exports and imports increased by 80 per cent more than output.

Something more than free trade and American benevolence however is required to explain the growth pattern of postwar Europe. The extra something was the adoption by nearly all countries of Keynesian policies. One author has described what happened as follows:[3]

> United States aid and balance of payments deficits would almost certainly have been insufficient in maintaining the growth momentum of the reconstruction period and in raising investment propensities in a world in which many

feared a quick relapse into stagnation or run-away inflation. What probably intervened was a new confidence factor instilled by the pressure of 'a bigger and better' government.

In other words, Keynesian measures to maintain the level of activity and employment had a doubly beneficial impact. They were valuable not only for their actual effect (which was considerable) but also because of the belief that governments could and would intervene to preserve growth. It gave industry the confidence to invest and go on investing. The European 'growth miracle' of the 1950s and 1960s was based, at least in part, on the conviction that Keynesian policies worked.

WHAT WENT WRONG

Why did the economic climate change in the 1970s ?

The fashionable monetarist explanation was that, in the 1970s, the Western industrial countries were paying the price for what happened in the 1950s and 1960s.[4] According to this philosophy, economies are basically self-stabilising and governments should limit themselves to balancing the budget and controlling the growth of the money supply in a way consistent with stable prices. Attempting to stimulate economic activity beyond the levels set by the 'natural rates of unemployment' cannot have more than a temporary effect. In the longer run, it is argued, it cannot change the volume of production but only the prices which people pay for what is produced. This increase in the rate of inflation will soon result in unemployment moving back up to and temporarily beyond the natural rate; any attempt to prevent this by further injections of purchasing power to increase demand will merely lead to a further increase in inflation. So, in the eyes of the monetarists, the recession of the 1970s was the inevitable consequence of the Keynesianism of the 1950s and 1960s.

However the monetarist explanation does not begin to provide a convincing explanation for what actually happened in the 1970s. It is true that, by the end of the 1960s, the OECD inflation rate had climbed to nearly 5 per cent. This was due in part to the inflationary financing of the Vietnam War and in part to the wage explosions of the late 1960s, following the events of 1968. But there is no proof that this short-term quickening in the rate of price increases was caused by Keynesian policies or led inexorably to what happened in 1973.

As far as the impact of Keynesian policies is concerned, most studies have discounted the importance of demand pressures and monetary expansion in the European wage explosions of the late 1960s.[5] It is also noticeable that the countries with the highest growth rates and lowest unemployment rates, (like Japan and West Germany) tended to have the lowest relative price increases. In any case, by 1972 inflation had moderated (though rather less in Western Europe than in the United States and Japan): the inflation rate for the seven major OECD countries in 1972 was 4.4 per cent, only 0.3 per cent higher than it had been in 1968. It was during 1973 that prices rocketed: in 1974 the rate for the seven major OECD countries was over 13 per cent or three times the rate in 1972. In short, 1973 represented a break rather than a progressive trend.

The analysis of the McCracken Committee of independent experts provides a much more satisfactory explanation. They concluded that the key factor in explaining what happened was 'an unusual bunching of unfortunate events unlikely to be repeated on the same scale, the impact of which was compounded by some avoidable errors in economic policy'.[6]

'The avoidable errors' in economic policy referred to in the McCracken Report were the speed and universality of the 1972-3 upswing and the excessive monetary expansion which led so quickly to production bottlenecks, shortages of raw materials, and steeply rising prices for commodities as buyers scrambled for supplies. The 1972-3 boom, with all the major OECD countries expanding at the same time, was the most rapid expansion since the 1950s. Between the first halves of 1972 and 1973, OECD GNP rose in real terms by 7½ per cent and industrial production by 10 per cent.

At the same time, the breakdown of the Bretton Woods system of fixed exchange rates (and the size of the United States payment deficit) precipitated an exceptional movement of funds into international capital markets which rapidly fed through into the domestic money supply in many countries. There was a big rise in prices of property and gold (markets which are traditional havens for foot-loose funds) and a speculative element was added to commodity dealing , already stimulated by the upswing and harvest failures.

Then, at the end of 1973, came the first oil price rises, following the outbreak of war in the Middle East. Between October 1973 and January 1974 the export price of oil increased by four times. This increase in the price of oil directly added $65 billion to the OECD oil bill; raised OECD prices by 2 per cent; and, most significantly of all, transferred from the OECD areas and the non-oil developing countries to OPEC and amount of real income equivalent to about 2 per cent of OECD GNP. This transfer not only hit the OECD countries directly but also reduced world demand, because OPEC had a lower marginal propensity to spend than the OECD and non-oil developing countries.[7] The effect of the oil increase was therefore both inflationary and deflationary – and it was hardly surprising that its impact has been described as a 'shock'.

So the inflationary upsurge of 1973 was not the final stage of a progressive trend upwards caused by twenty years of misguided Keynesian policies but the consequence of an uncontrolled economic upswing in 1972-3, excessive monetary expansion (following the breakdown of Bretton Woods), and the impact of the first oil shock. Whether this 'unusual bunching of unfortunate events' and, in particular, the oil 'shock', would also lead to recession, unemployment and lower growth, depended on the response of policy-makers.

THE RESPONSE TO THE FIRST OIL SHOCK

At the beginning of 1974, the Western countries were faced with difficult policy dilemmas. On the one hand, the impact of a quadrupling in the cost of oil on the level of inflation and the balance of trade was only too obvious. On the other hand, the demand effect of the forced transfer of income to the OPEC countries had also to be considered. If the level of activity was to be maintained, OECD countries would have to accept their current account deficits. Otherwise there would be a fall in the level of world income and output and a substantial increase in unemployment.

The initial response to these policy dilemmas suggested that they would be solved within a Keynesian framework. Ministers of Finance meeting in Rome in January 1974 under the auspices of the IMF's Committee of Twenty stressed the importance of sustaining the level of world activity and agreed that current account deficits should be accepted for the time being. But, as it turned out, the policy response was uneven.

The three biggest OECD countries – the United States, Japan and West Germany – gave priority to reducing inflation and the balance of payments deficits. In the United States, monetary policy was tightened considerably, while fiscal policy became increasingly restrictive. In Japan, similar policies were pursued. As a consequence, output in both countries fell dramatically and the balance of payments swung into surplus. In other words, policy had compounded rather than compensated for the deflationary effects of the oil price rise.[8]

From the point of view of Socialists, the behaviour of West Germany, under an SPD–Liberal coalition, was especially significant. Accustomed to balances of payments surpluses and, for historical reasons, more sensitive to the inflationary rather than deflationary implications of the oil shock, the West German Government adopted a restrictive approach. In response to the inflationary upswing of 1972–3, a severe deflationary package had already been adopted in May 1973 and, although a number of stimulating measures were introduced during 1974, monetary policy remained tight. As a result, unemployment rose from about 1 per cent in the middle of 1973 to about 5 per cent in the middle of 1975 (the latter figure did not include the large number of guest workers from Southern Europe). The surplus on the balance of payments increased from less than $2 billion to a staggering $10 billion. In this way, the policies of a country whose economy was particularly dependent on an expanding world economy reinforced rather than mitigated international deflationary pressures.

Ironically, the success of West German exporters relied on other countries adopting strategies which were more consistent with the January 1974 statement of Finance Ministers. Britain, with a new Labour Government, Italy and, amongst smaller countries, Sweden and Austria, made deliberate attempts to sustain the level of demand. France followed an intermediate policy – maintaining output until mid-1974, followed by a tight squeeze later in the year.

The consequence of this varied response was the 1974–5 recession, the sharpest since the war. There was a severe drop in investment and a dramatic reduction in stocks, as well as a drop in consumption, partly due to an increase in personal savings. It was clear that the confidence of businessmen and consumers, such an important factor in the growth of the previous twenty years, collapsed very quickly when governments showed themselves uncertain how to deal with the new conditions. Industrial production fell by 10 per cent between July 1974 and April 1975, and by the second quarter of 1975 unemployment in OECD countries had risen from a low of some 8 million during the 1972–3 boom to around 15 million or 5½ per cent of the workforce – a postwar record.

By the end of 1975 the OECD economy began to move out of recession. During 1975 a number of countries, including West Germany, France and Italy as well as the United States, Japan and Canada, shifted their fiscal policies in a more expansionary direction, so that by the beginning of 1976 growth had been resumed. But the recovery remained fragile. During 1976 the three main European countries (West Germany, France and the United Kingdom) switched back to a more cautious budgetary posture. The EEC Commission's explanation of this caution was that 'after the recovery process had weakened in the latter half of 1976, policy-makers continued to be restrained by high budget deficits, inflationary pressures and, in some countries, weak currencies, to maintain at best an overall neutral posture.'[9]

A new factor was the concern over the budget deficits. It is true that public sector deficits had climbed to an average of over 4 per cent of GNP in the seven major OECD countries. But these deficits were to a great extent caused by the recession itself – by reduced tax yields and by the increases in spending on unemployment and other benefits. And, at a time when unemployment was still high, resources idle, and private investment low, it made good sense for a government to run a budget deficit.

However, there was growing support amongst international banking opinion for the monetarist argument that budget deficits were either inflationary (if they were financed through the banking system) or would somehow lead to the 'crowding out' of private investment (if they were financed by borrowing from the non-bank private sector). And, in an era of floating exchange rates, competitive interest rates, large OPEC surpluses and hyper-active Eurocurrency markets, the views of those who controlled vast sums of money which could be rapidly switched from one country or currency to another were increasingly important.

They were certainly influential in the crisis over British economic policy leading to the IMF agreement in December 1976. As we have seen above, the new Labour Government had tried to keep up the level of activity. However, the balance of payments deficit, swollen by the deflationary policies of other countries, remained large, and inflation was rising. Ironically it was only in 1976, when it was clear that the incomes policy introduced in 1975 was proving extremely efficient in reducing inflation and that the balance of payments deficit had been halved, that there was a real loss of confidence in sterling.

As well as believing that the British Labour Government had decided on depreciation, the international financial community had also made up its mind that public spending in Britain was out of control, even though (as later figures showed) the public sector borrowing requirement had already fallen. Britain was forced to call in the IMF and accept cuts in planned public spending of £1½ million in 1977–8 and £2–2½ million in 1978–9. One author has accurately summed up the British experiment as follows:

> What happened in 1976 was that a major industrial country was forced, because of the disapproval of its mildly social-democratic and expansionist policies felt by the world financial community and a business-orientated regime in Washington, to apply for a loan and to accept terms for the loan that seemed at the time to be very close to national humiliation.[10]

If 1976 and 1977 were bad years for Keynesianism, 1978 was much more encouraging. The continuing high level of unemployment and slow growth rates throughout the OECD area led to pressure on those countries which (like West Germany and Japan) had managed to reestablish a strong balance of payments to take concerted budgetary action to assist world recovery. At the Bonn summit of 1978, both Japan and West Germany announced substantial reflationary packages, while other countries, including France, Italy and Canada, also agreed to raise their growth rate. This international initiative had a significant impact. Output growth, which had fallen to 2 per cent in 1977, rose to 4 per cent by the end of 1978 and the recovery continued well into 1979.

In view of what followed, it is worth remembering that a concerted expansionist policy, with the stronger countries taking the lead, actually worked effectively in the late 1970s. It was the second oil shock in 1979 (following the overthrow of the Shah of Iran) which brought this experiment in international coordination to a premature conclusion.

THE SECOND OIL SHOCK

The second oil shock, which took 2 per cent of GNP out of the OECD economy, was very similar in its deflationary impact to the first. But the response showed how much the political and economic climate had changed. The United States, under pressure because of her balance of payments deficit, engineered a severe deflation. The European countries adopted a similar posture. The new Conservative Government firmly rejected Keynesian policies and, despite growing recession, embarked on a succession of deflationary budgets. The French administration under Barre was committed to an equally restrictive approach. Even the West German Government, which had taken the lead in international expansion a year earlier, was not prepared to risk going it alone. As one author wrote, 'economic virtue 1979–80 style consisted in each nation giving its full attention to looking after its own backyard on the lines indicated by a common and fairly severe monetary drill book'.[11] An OECD paper summed up the response in a similar way: 'Rather than seeking to support demand, the overriding concern, felt by virtually all OECD Governments, was to contain the inflationary impulse and to prevent, through a rapid re-adjustment of real wages, the price shock becoming built into the domestic wage/price spiral.'[12]

In fact, between 1979 and 1982, so far from supporting demand the main OECD countries, by their fiscal and monetary restrictions, actually added a further 3 per cent to the 2 per cent deflationary impact caused by the oil price rise.[13] Though there was a significant reduction in inflation, there was also a prolonged depression of output and investment and rising unemployment, particularly in Europe. Faced by the admittedly difficult problems caused by the second oil shock, almost all the

OECD governments abandoned Keynesian economic policies and seemed prepared to accept indefinitely much higher levels of unemployment and much lower levels of growth.

One country, France, under the incoming Socialist Government, tried to break out of recession on her own. Pledged to bring down unemployment, the new Government introduced a mildly expansionist policy in 1981. But, in an open trading system, it was extremely difficult for France to pursue expansion whilst the other countries were contracting their economies, without also running into balance of payments problems and coming under pressure from the world financial markets. By March 1983, the French Socialist Government, like the British Labour Government in 1976, had been forced to abandon its growth strategy. The monetarist view seemed again to have triumphed.

CONCLUSION

But if monetarists triumphed in the short term, it was a pyrrhic victory. As the consequence of the adoption of deflationary policies in many OECD countries, and particularly in the United States and the United Kingdom, output fell and unemployment rose far more rapidly and strongly than the monetarists anticipated. It is true that inflation had been reduced but in 1985 it was much the same as the rate of the late 1960s and the early 1970s. Unemployment in Western Europe was over 11 per cent, while the levels of growth and investment, particularly in Western Europe, were much lower than in the 1960s. The simplistic monetarist view that economies were self-stabilising began to seem untenable, even to former adherents.

In a few countries, faith in the effectiveness of government action had not been lost. Throughout the years of recession, Austria, under a Socialist government pursuing Keynesian policies, combined low inflation with low unemployment and high growth. Sweden also managed to maintain a low unemployment level which the returning Social Democrat Government preserved by introducing a major devaluation in 1982 which boosted exports, investment and output. Ironically, the United States, under a Republican President committed to slashing public spending, also successfully expanded its economy by the classical Keynesian method of increasing its budget deficit. Unemployment in the United States fell rapidly, whilst the rate of inflation remained stable. Not surprisingly, the Republican President was reelected in 1984.

However, although monetary policies have clearly been seen to have failed and some countries have successfully adopted full employment strategies, there were two features of modern industrial economies which made European decision-makers less confident about pursuing Keynessian policies in the mid-1980s than they were in the 1950s and 1960s.

The first is unregulated collective bargaining. It was difficult to argue, particularly after the inflationary upsurge of 1973, that wages were the only or even always the predominant cause of inflation. On the other hand, settlements which far outstrip output and productivity (as in the 1974-5 wages round in Britain) could clearly be an important factor. Obviously, during recession, wage-generated inflation was less likely. But policy-makers in a number of countries believed, with some justice, that there was a danger that when expansion was resumed and labour's negotiating power strengthened, over-aggressive bargaining could first distort and then choke off the upswing. It is certainly worth noting that those countries, like Austria and Sweden, which have been best able to combine low unemployment with low inflation, also have the most constructive relationships between government and unions.

The other facet of modern industrial economies which is of even greater significance for Keynesian policies is their growing interdependence. As has been pointed out, over the past twenty years world trade has risen considerably faster than output. Most OECD countries have experienced a sharp increase in the proportion of their GDP represented by imports and exports. Nowhere has this shift gone further than in Europe. By the mid-1970s most Western European countries were exporting up to a quarter of their total output (in the case of the Benelux countries, the proportion was 50 per cent). There has also been a big increase in international lending and borrowing (partly as a consequence of the two oil shocks) and the availability of short-term capital has become much greater.

The implication of this interdependence is that the ability of governments to influence their own output and employment has been weakened and their vulnerability to outside events and pressure has been increased. This change is of great importance to Keynesians, not merely for theoretical reasons but because, as it operated in the 1980s, the international economy had a deflationary bias. When a particular country adopted a restrictive stance, its impact was likely to affect the output of others. On the other hand, when a country adopted expansionist policies, the result was less likely to be the transmission of expansion than the discouragement of those policies by fiscally conservative international financial institutions and by more orthodox governments.

We have seen above that medium-size economies which attempted to expand against the trend, like the United Kingdom in the mid-1970s and France in the early 1980s, were unsuccessful. Both ran up large balance of payments deficits and, because of loss of reserves, were forced to succumb to the pressure of other governments and the international bankers, and change their policies. West Germany, the most powerful European economy, was prepared to expand in 1978 in agreement with other countries but did not consider continuing that expansion when conditions changed after the second oil shock. In part, this was because of purely national considerations. But the restrictive policies of other countries, particularly the United States and the United Kingdom, made reflation far more problematic. Even the United States, the world's greatest economy, sometimes found it difficult to go it alone, or at least to maintain a policy out of synchronisation with that of the others. At the end of the 1970s, after several years of expansion, the American authorities (in contrast to their attitude in the 1950s and 1960s) were so worried by the United States balance of payments deficit and by currency speculation, that they also contracted their economy. During the American expansion of the 1980s, the United States Government was under pressure from other governments because of its high interest rates.

Paradoxically, some smaller countries, in part because of their size, were able to shift or maintain policy against the trend. As we have seen, the Austrians were able to keep up a high pressure of demand throughout the recession, and the incoming Social Democratic Government in Sweden was able to bring off a major devaluation in 1982, largely because Sweden was not economically important enough to force other major countries to take similar action.

If much of the evidence pointed to the necessity for concerted action by the industrial countries, there were also considerable problems, partly economic and partly political, which made such concerted action difficult to achieve. The 1978–9 expansion following the Bonn Summit was an example of successful coordination. But the ill-fated 1972–3 boom was a severe warning of the dangers of too ambitious an expansion by too many countries at once. It was clear that an international initiative had to be carefully planned and synchronised. But for such a comparatively complex exercise to succeed, there had to be considerable self-confidence, mutual trust and, above all, the belief among the trading of the larger economies that such coordinated action was likely to be successful. In the 1970s first the United States and then West Germany and Japan tried to lead the world out of recession and failed. Inevitably, these failures left their mark on the 1980s so that, despite the success of the Keynesian expansion in the United States and the considerable combined economic power of the biggest European economies, there is still not the will to act effectively together. Perhaps the fall in the price of oil which started at the end of 1985 and which has so improved economic prospects will make coordination easy to achieve.

Part II
The Politics of Recession

3 The SPD: Success, Setback and Revival

The German Social Democrats were, in many ways, the best placed of the Socialist parties in power to cope with and withstand the recession. In 1972 the Social Democrat/Free Democrat coalition had won a resounding victory and, although the Christian Democrats remained a powerful force, the alliance with the Free Democrats was likely to continue to give the left of centre coalition the edge. The change of leadership was also beneficial, as Helmut Schmidt was probably better equipped to be the Chancellor of the 'bad times' than Willy Brandt. Most important of all, the German economy was the strongest in Europe – an inestimable advantage to the Social Democrats. This chapter examines the response of the Social Democrats to the two oil shocks and assesses their political record and prospects.

HELMUT SCHMIDT: CHANCELLOR OF THE 'BAD TIMES'

Schmidt was a highly intelligent and experienced politician who was well qualified to lead Germany in the unfavourable environment of the 1970s. He had made his political reputation as an extremely successful Senator for Internal Affairs in his native Hamburg and as the SPD floor leader in the Bundestag during the period of the grand coalition. In Brandt's first administration, Schmidt was a competent Minister of Defence and after 1972 became first Minister of Economics and Finance and then Minister of Finance.

A self-confessed pragmatist who defined politics 'as pragmatic action for moral purposes or moral ends' and believed strongly that political action must be 'preceded by a critical analysis of the situation and of the context',[1] Schmidt nevertheless understood that moderation and caution had to be balanced by adaptability and creativity. Under Schmidt, the coalition's approach to the first recession was an eclectic amalgam of Keynesian fiscal measures, monetary control, a strong currency policy, moderate wage settlements, labour market interventionism and an integrationist social strategy.

It has sometimes been incorrectly argued, especially by British Conservatives, that Schmidt was a monetarist. It is certainly true that, throughout his Chancellorship, the independent Bundesbank gave priority to control over the money supply. However, even the Bundesbank, often rightly criticised for restrictive policies, was prepared to react flexibly to changing conditions, as was shown in 1975 and in 1977–8.

More significantly, throughout the 1970s, the coalition Government used the federal budget counter-cyclically to assist expansion and employment and give help to industry. During 1974 three programmes amounting to DM 3.6 billion of additional public spending (mainly on housing, energy saving and labour market projects) as well as a 7½ per cent subsidy for immediate industrial investment were announced; while in 1975 in addition to a package of tax reductions and child allowance increases which came into effect in January, a further DM 5.7 billion, concentrated on public construction works, was introduced. In 1977 a medium-term public investment programme of DM 13.8 billion over four years as well as a number of tax concessions was launched; and in 1978, after the Bonn summit, a DM 12 billion immediate expansion plan was approved. In part as a result of these measures (though there were other factors, including the impact of the recession) the general government deficit rose from 1.4 per cent in 1974 to 3 per cent in 1979, while total government expenditure went up from 37.6 per cent of GNP in 1970 to 47 per cent in 1980.[2]

With respect to inflation (of great importance for Germans psychologically as well as economically) the Bundesbank monetary approach, as well as the maintenance of a strong mark, obviously assisted in creating a favourable climate. But the key factor was the moderate level of wage settlements from 1975 onwards. In theory there was no incomes policy; in practice German bargainers paid very close attention to the views of SPD ministers on the kind of wage increases which the economy could afford. There was, in fact, a highly successful, if unwritten, 'social contract' between government and unions.

In part, this relationship was based on the close ties between trade unions and the SPD. As the 1972 election had shown, trade unionists believed that the coalition was *their* government. But it was not only a matter of sentiment. An SPD-led coalition, committed to protecting employment, was clearly preferable to a CDU-led coalition. In the more difficult conditions of post-oil shock Germany, Schmidt did not feel in a position to extend substantially the Brandt social reforms (see Chapter 10 for a discussion of the Schmidt government's social record). There were, however, two areas of importance to the unions in which the Schmidt Government was able to make significant advances.

In labour market policy, there were some major initiatives, particularly in the introduction of employment creation schemes to help young workers, and in the expansion of vocational training. In 1976 a Training Opportunities Act was passed which, over a four-year period, helped increase training places from 450 000 to 630 000 a year. The Government also carried through the Bundestag legislation which introduced a 'parity' system of co-determination (albeit in a weakened form) on the supervisory boards of all companies employing over 2000 workers – a reform for which the unions had long fought. For their part, the powerful and highly centralised German trade unions 'delivered' on moderate wage settlements.

Although it was highly dependent on imported energy (and therefore all the more vulnerable to increases in energy prices), the German economy recovered quicker from the first oil shock than her main European competitors. In 1974 there was little growth in output, unemployment climbed to 4 per cent, and the inflation rate rose to 7 per cent, high by German standards. But by the third quarter of 1975 a strong upswing was apparent. In 1976 GNP grew by 5.7 per cent, unemployment had stabilised at 3.9 per cent (though without a reduction in the numbers of foreign workers it would have been higher) and the inflation level had fallen to 3.9 per cent.[3]

In the previous chapter we have already seen that Germany's rapid recovery after 1973 was due in part to two factors. First, the coalition put the preservation of a low inflation rate and getting the balance of payments back into surplus before full employment. Before the first oil shock, the government had already introduced a deflationary budget and, despite the rise in unemployment, did not shift to a more expansionary position until 1975. Second, the Government relied on other governments expanding their home markets and thus opening up opportunities for German exporters. To some extent, it was the Keynesian policies of other governments, allied to Germany's lower inflation rate, which helped expand the German economy and bring down German unemployment, while at the same time protecting the German balance of payments. In the short term, it was a highly successful policy for West Germany, if considerably less helpful to other countries.

Understandably, the SPD made the most of these achievements during the 1976 election campaign. It campaigned on the slogan *Modell Deutschland*, emphasing not only Germany's superior economic record but also showing how this was linked to the social cohesion which Schmidt and his ministers had worked so hard to sustain. In the circumstances, the result of the election was a good one for the coalition. Although the SPD lost a million votes and dropped from 45.8 per cent to 42.6 per cent of the total poll, the coalition parties still had an overall majority of ten. And, despite an increased share of the vote, the CDU's failure to topple Schmidt was a serious setback which the party took some time to get over. The 1976 election also confirmed and enhanced Schmidt's personal position. In the next four years, he dominated West German politics.

MODELL DEUTSCHLAND

During 1977, Schmidt handled the threat of terrorism with coolness, efficiency and moderation. He refused to capitulate to the demands of the Red Army Faction after the kidnapping of the German industrialist, Hans Martin Schleyer. He took a leading role in directing the operation which freed the Lufthansa hostages at Mogadishu in Somalia. And the new counter-terrorist measures introduced by the Government, though they gave the police increased powers, were less extensive than in many other Western states. The chancellor's reputation as a successful crisis manager and guardian of German democracy grew both at home and abroad.

Schmidt's preeminence as Chancellor coincided with the emergence in the mid-1970s of the Federal Republic as what one commentator has described as a 'European Great Power'.[4] West Germany was the strategic outpost of the NATO alliance with the largest conventional forces in Western Europe. In the heyday of detente she was also the main bridge between Eastern and Western Europe. Perhaps most important of all was Germany's new economic strength. It was a power which was severely circumscribed. After all, German success was relative. She might have done better than her European rivals in the post-oil shock world. But her GNP was still only a third of that of the USA and smaller than that of Japan. And, as the world's largest exporter after the USA, she was heavily dependent on the state of the world economy and, as one of the major importers of energy, on the decisions of Opec.

Schmidt never made the mistake of overestimating German power[5]. As a Social Democrat of the war generation, he was also understandably chary of independent German initiatives. He preferred to act in concert with his European partners (particularly France), with Germany's major ally, the United States, and with the other major OECD countries. But he saw no alternative to a greater German role, particularly in international economic affairs. If the lesson of 1974-5 was that West Germany's prosperity and growth was increasingly dependent on the world economy, then it became a German interest to see that it operated more effectively.

West Germany played a major part in the summit meetings of the major OECD countries; in response to the demand for concerted action, Schmidt agreed at the London conference in May 1977 to a 5 per cent growth target for the German economy and, in the following year, after the Bonn conference in July, the coalition pledged itself to measures amounting to an extra 1 per cent growth in GNP. As a country running a balance of payments surplus, Schmidt was prepared to accept that West Germany had an obligation to expand somewhat faster than most of her competitors. In return, however, he insisted that the commitment to free trade, so important to an exporting nation, be reaffirmed.

The West German Chancellor was also concerned about the instability of the world monetary system, following the collapse of the Bretton Woods structure in 1972, and was the prime mover in the establishment in March 1979 of the European Monetary System (EMS), whose main purpose was the creation of a zone of monetary stability within Europe. From West Germany's point of view, a mark which was less susceptible to short-term pressures upwards would favour export industries, while her economy as a whole could benefit from the limits to competitive devaluation laid down by the rules of the EMS.

In addition, the SPD/FDP coalition took seriously its responsibilities in the North/South dialogue. It was no accident that Willy Brandt, former Chancellor and chairman of the SPD and the Socialist International, chaired the Independent Commission on International Development Issues which published its celebrated report in 1980. Schmidt too was well aware of the plight of the less-developed countries and of the interdependence between North and South. Between 1976 and 1980, when other countries were cutting back, the Federal Republic increased its development aid to 0.44 per cent of GNP, which brought it into second place, with France, among donor countries. It also pursued a liberal policy towards imported industrial products from developing countries and was a strong supporter of the 2nd Lomé convention, linking the EEC with sixty countries of Africa, the Caribbean and the Pacific.

The result of the 1980 election, in which the coalition gained thirty-five seats, was a personal triumph for Schmidt. He fought the election as a major world statesman who, unlike his controversial CDU/CSU challenger, Franz-Joseph Strauss, could be trusted to guide his country in the difficult years of the 1980s. A common post-electoral assessment was that, in the words of a *Financial Times* headline, 'Schmidt wins more elbow room'.[6] In fact, the next two years saw the decline and fall of the Schmidt Chancellorship and the breakup of the SPD/FDP coalition.

THE FALL OF THE SCHMIDT GOVERNMENT

There were a number of reasons for this turn of events. The SPD leadership seemed to tire.[7] Schmidt himself suffered from ill health and had to have a heart pacemaker operation in October 1981. The party was split over policy. Although the executive and the congress continued to support Schmidt's so-called 'twin track' policy on theatre nuclear weapons (Western deployment combined with negotiations with Moscow) and his position on nuclear energy, there was a vociferous minority which was implacably opposed to the siting of cruise missiles. There was also a growing feeling among party activists that the compromises inevitable in a coalition government were all made by the SPD and that a period in opposition after over fifteen years in power might be no bad thing for the party.

This unrest in the SPD coincided with a new assertiveness by its coalition partner, following its gains in the 1980 elections. While the SDP had only increased its share of the vote by 0.3 per cent, the FDP had gone up from 7.9 per cent to 10.5 per cent of the vote – its best result since 1961. The two parties had difficulty in reaching agreement over the common legislative programme in November 1980 and there were bitter disputes over the shape and size of the budget in both 1981 and 1982 which revealed a crucial difference of approach in how to deal with the deterioriation in West Germany's economic position.

The combination of the 1979 oil shock and the Government's response to it had a severe impact on the economy. It is true that the inflation rate remained one of the lowest in the OECD and that the balance of payments after several years in deficit returned to balance during 1982. But in contrast to the middle 1970s, these successes were achieved at the expense of output and employment. In 1980 GNP rose by only 1.8 per cent and in 1981 and 1982 it actually fell by .2 per cent, and 1.2 per cent respectively – the first time in West German history that GNP had fallen for two consecutive years. Unemployment rose sharply. In September 1979 it was under 800 000 and only 3.2 per cent of the labour force: by October 1982 it had climbed to over 2 million and had risen to 7.5 per cent of the labour force.[8]

Why was the SPD/FDP coalition so much less successful in dealing with the second oil shock than it was with the first? It was partly that the underlying factors – both external and internal – were less favourable than in 1974–5. With an economy so heavily dependent on imported oil, West Germany remained especially vulnerable to oil price increases. In 1972 6 per cent of her exports could pay for her entire oil bill. In the conditions of 1974–5 West Germany had been able to boost her exports rapidly not only to cover the increased cost of her fuel imports but also to help lead her economy out of recession. But in the years following 1979, governments which, like those of the USA and the UK, had reflated in 1974–5 (thus assisting German exports) pursued far more restrictive policies. As a consequence, world trade slowed down drastically and, despite the depreciation of the mark against the dollar, this deterioration undermined the prospects for a West German export strategy similar to 1974–5.

A domestic reflation was also more difficult to achieve than in 1974–5. With American interest rates so high, the Bundesbank also kept German interest rates much higher than was justified by internal developments. And, whereas in 1973 the budget was in surplus, in 1980 the deficit was over 3 per cent of GNP. Even so, it should have been possible to introduce more substantial counter-cyclical measures during 1981 and in 1982.

One reason for the failure to take action was that the West German Government underestimated the depth of the international recession. Another important factor, however, was the differences within the coalition between the FDP and the SPD. The FDP Economics Minister, Count Otto Lambsdorff, insisted on a strategy which gave priority to keeping down inflation, bringing the balance of payments into surplus and reducing the budget deficit at the expense of output and employment. The SPD, particularly the parliamentary party, argued for more public investment and employment measures and was deeply disappointed when in September 1981 the FDP vetoed a DM 1 billion job creation programme and insisted on a restrictive federal budget for 1982.

As unemployment rose and output fell, as the coalition partners squabbled and the SPD grumbled, public discontent with the performance of the Government grew. In the May 1981 elections in Berlin, in the Land elections in Lower Saxony in March 1982 and in Hamburg in June 1982, the SPD lost votes to the CDU, particularly amongst its working-class constituency. Acording to the public opinion polls, its support had slipped to little over 30 per cent, its lowest share since the 1960s. In addition, the SPD was also losing young middle-class votes to the Greens, the loose anti-nuclear, pro-environmental grouping which, in contrast to the FDP, was able to surmount the 5 per cent barrier to gain representation in a number of Land parliaments. At the same time, trade union criticism of the government's economic policy for the first time became vocal – always a warning signal.

It was against this deteriorating economic and political background that it became increasingly obvious that the FDP leaders, Genscher and Lambsdorff, concerned about their party's declining fortunes, were making preparations to desert the SPD after the

Hesse elections in September 1982 and form a new coalition with the CDU/CSU. Rather than wait for a lingering death, Schmidt decided that the Government would fall at a time and on an issue which was more favourable to the SPD. As his response to a document written by Lambsdorff which called for a new austerity package, including cuts in social welfare, Schmidt sacked the FDP ministers and called for immediate elections. Although a new coalition, under the CDU leader, Helmut Kohl, was formed and elections delayed until March 1983, support for the SPD's action in going into opposition was shown by its improved performance in the Hesse, Bavarian and Hamburg elections.

1983–5: SETBACK AND RECOVERY

Following Schmidt's decision to stand down, the Social Democrats fought the March 1983 general election under a new candidate for Chancellor, Hans Jochen Vogel, the former Justice minister. But, despite an energetic campaign, the SPD polled only 38.2 per cent of the vote – its worst result since 1961. The party lost some middle-class support to the Greens, which, with 5.6 per cent entered the Bundestag for the first time, and even more working-class votes to the CDU/CSU, which won 48.8 per cent (the second best result in its history). The position of Kohl's Centre–Right coalition was significantly strengthened and the SPD, after nearly sixteen years in power, had now to get used to opposition.

On the whole, the Social Democrats managed the transition with skill. At the Cologne Congress in November 1983, the party, encouraged by its Chairman, Willy Brandt, over-whelmingly rejected Schmidt's 'two-track' strategy and voted against the deployment of Cruise and Pershing missiles on German soil. But thanks mainly to Schmidt's dignified behaviour in defeat, this change in position took place without rancour. And, although Vogel lacked popular appeal, he was effective in keeping the party together.

In May 1985 the political climate began to shift in the SPD's favour. Chancellor Kohl's complacent and lacklustre performance in office, tax scandals which implicated the coalition parties, as well as persistently high unemployment, provided the ideal background for the SPD's campaign in the largest state, North Rhine Westphalia. Johannes Rau, the State Prime minister was triumphantly reelected with 52.1 per cent of the vote. In September Rau, boosted by this result and by favourable public opinion polls, agreed to be considered as the party's candidate for Chancellor.

At the end of 1985, the Social Democrats looked forward to the 1987 federal elections with much more enthusiasm than had appeared possible at the beginning of the year. In Rau they had a candidate who was likely to prove a considerable electoral asset. The SPD was running neck and neck with the Christian Democrats in the polls. And Kohl's coalition had so far failed to make much impression on unemployment.

However, there were still formidable obstacles to overcome. Unless the party could win outright, it would find it difficult to put together a governing coalition. The FDP, which had so cruelly undermined the Schmidt Government in 1982, had ruled themselves out as coalition partners for the time being. The 'Greens', whose future in the Bundestag was in any case in doubt, had already revealed themselves as unreliable bedfellows at state level. A grand coalition with the Christian Democrats might have been appropriate in the 1960s, but seemed anachronistic in the late 1980s. So, despite a remarkable recovery, there was some way to go on the road back to power.

CONCLUSION

The period of Helmut Schmidt's Chancellorship (1974–82) covered the difficult years of the world recession. German recovery from the first oil shock was quicker than most of her competitors. As a result, the SPD-led coalition, with Schmidt as the dominant figure, won both the 1976 and 1980 elections, while externally the influence of Germany increased considerably. After 1980 the relatively less successful response to the second oil shock helped undermine Schmidt's Chancellorship and was a major factor in the downfall of the coalition in September 1982 and in the subsequent defeat of the Social Democrats in March 1983. However, the SPD remained formidable in opposition and by the end of 1985 were beginning to mount a fresh challenge for power.

4 The French Socialist Experiment: From Expansion to Austerity

The French Socialists fought the presidential and parliamentary elections of 1981 on the promise to expand output and bring down unemployment. However, their attempt to stimulate the French economy was checked in June 1982 and then brought to a halt in March 1983. This chapter considers how the experiment of 'reflation in one country' failed, how the French Socialist government, against its will, was forced to change direction and how, despite remaining the largest party in the National Assembly, it lost the 1986 parliamentary elections.

THE PATH TO VICTORY

When on 10 May François Mitterrand beat Valèry Giscard d'Estaing by 51.76 per cent to 48.24 per cent, it was the first time in French political history that a left-wing President had been elected by universal suffrage. The overall majority gained by the French Socialists on the second ballot of 21 June was also the first time that the Socialists had ever been in a majority in the National Assembly. It was a historic victory.

The French Socialists had come a long way in a short time. Under the Fourth Republic, the Socialists had been in a decline, very much the junior party of the Left, behind the Communists (PCF). In the second presidential election of the Fifth Republic in 1969, Gaston Deferre, the Socialist candidate, had only mustered a humiliating 5 per cent of the vote. The Socialist renaissance began in 1971 when a reconstituted Socialist party, the *Parti Socialiste* (PS), was set up at Epinay under the leadership of François Mitterrand.

Mitterrand's strategy was to win power both by uniting the Left, and by ensuring that the Socialists were supreme within that union. He knew from his own experience in 1965 as the candidate of the Left against De Gaulle (when he received 44.8 per cent of the votes) that, under the existing constitution of the Fifth Republic, the only way a candidate of the Left could win the Presidency was with the support of Communist votes. On the other hand, it was quite clear that the Communists, even with official Socialist backing, could never win. If it was to be successful, the union of the Left had to be led by the Socialists.

In June 1972, the Socialists and the Communists signed an agreement on policy, the Common Programme, which committed the two parties to a major extension of public ownership and ambitious social welfare reforms. The Communists, led by Georges Marchais, saw the accord with the Socialists as helping them out of the political ghetto. For his part, Mitterrand believed that the union of the Left would assist the Socialists to become the major party of the Left. He told leaders of the Socialist International that 'our basic objective is to rebuild a great Socialist party on the territory now occupied by the Communists and thus to show that of five million Communist voters, three million can be brought to vote Socialist'.[1]

Left-wing politics in the years between June 1972 and the Socialist victory in 1981 were shaped by the rivalry between the Socialists and the Communists. The PS, a loose alliance of different Socialist factions and groupings, proved itself capable of attracting support across the class and political spectrum. At a specially convened *Assises du Socialisme*, held in the autumn of 1974, the PS welcomed an influx of new members from the smaller *Partie Socialiste Unifie* (PSU) led by Michel Rocard, as well as a smaller group from the Centre Left, including Jacques Delors.[2] Membership grew rapidly from 60 000 members in 1971 to nearly 200 000 by 1978. The first hard evidence that the Socialists had overtaken the Communists was provided by the Presidential election of 1974 when Mitterrand came within an ace of winning, polling 49.3 per cent of the vote to Giscard's 50.7 per cent. After that, the Socialists went from strength to strength. At both the 1976 cantonal elections and the 1977 municipal elections, the Socialists ran ahead of the Communists, pulling the Left to victory.

The expansion of the PS clearly presented a major challenge to the Communists. If the Left won the 1978 parliamentary elections, the Communists would be very much the junior partner in a government dominated by the Socialists and, after the 1977 Nantes conference of the PS, perhaps even by the heretical 'worker participation' policies of Rocard. The PCF leadership therefore decided to 'pull the rug' from under the Socialists by a barrage of public criticism and by demanding changes in the Common Programme which they knew that the Socialists could not accept. In September 1977 talks broke down over the Communist call for more nationalisation and the Left went into the March 1978 elections badly divided. Although a second ballot agreement was belatedly patched up (after the PS had polled only 2 per cent more than the PCF on the first ballot), the Left was narrowly defeated. The prospects for the 1981 Presidential election did not look good.

Two factors, however, turned the tide for the Socialists. The first was the economic and social policies of President Giscard. The economic background to the 1974 Presidential election had been helpful to Giscard. In 1973 gross domestic product had increased by 6 per cent and a fast rate of expansion continued during the first half of 1974. Unemployment was only 2.1 per cent and, though inflation was rising, the first oil shock took some time to move through the economy.[3] The Presidential election of 1981 took place in a much less favourable economic climate. From the end of the first quarter of 1980, gross domestic product and disposable incomes fell, and unemployment increased from 6.2 per cent to 7.8 per cent between November 1980 and October 1981. But despite the stagnation in the economy, inflation was 13.5 per cent in 1980 (higher than most of her competitors) and increased rapidly during 1981.[4]

The Socialists could argue, with considerable justification, that Giscard's economic policies had failed. It is true that, throughout the 1970s, the French economy maintained a growth rate of 3 per cent. But unemployment had trebled between 1973 and 1981 and the rate of investment had fallen, while the inflation rate never dropped much below 10 per cent. After 1976, Giscard gave priority to policies designed to curb inflation and reduce the balance of payments deficit. The plan, introduced by Raymond Barre, the Prime Minister and Finance Minister, included measures to balance the budget, as well as a temporary prices freeze and wage restraint. But, although the balance of payments position improved, inflation remained relatively high and unemployment continued to rise steadily. Then, from 1978,

Barre pursued a policy of improving corporate profitability by price liberalisation, increasing public utility prices and decontrolling the prices of industrial and consumer goods, while still maintaining a restrictive fiscal and monetary stance. Despite the second oil shock in 1979, Barre continued his policies – and growth, investment, living standards, employment all suffered accordingly, while inflation remained high.

The stagnation of the economy highlighted the divisions and disparities in French society. In the 1960s, when the French economy and French living standards were growing as fast as any country in Europe, it was politically possible for governments of the Right to ignore the dramatic inequalities in French society. In the 1970s it was far more difficult to sweep under the carpet the OECD report (published in mid-1976) which showed that France had the most unequal income distribution of the major industrial countries and that the social welfare system, instead of acting as a corrective, actually redistributed in favour of the better off.[5] Other studies of wealth, housing, education and social mobility in France confirmed the picture of a 'a rigidly stratified society in which the inequalities between social classes exceed, in almost all respects, those found in virtually any other industrial nation'.[6]

Secondly, the clumsy tactics of the Communist leadership also played into Socialists' hands and helped build up Mitterrand's candidacy. Marchais, who in October 1980 had been the first of the major candidates to declare himself, continued to make fierce attacks on the Socialists until the eve of the first ballot. However, on the first ballot the Communist vote plunged to 15 per cent – their worst result since 1936. A million or so Communist voters either abstained or voted for Mitterrand (whom they had, in any case, already supported in 1974) as the only Left candidate with a chance of beating Giscard. As a result, Mitterrand polled nearly 26 per cent on the first ballot, less than 6 per cent behind Giscard. Giscard was badly hurt by divisions in the governing majority. Jacques Chirac, leader of the Gaullist party (RPR) and Giscard's former prime minister, campaigned vigorously for his own candidature and his endorsement of Giscard on the second ballot was less than wholehearted.

After the first ballot result (with the Communist vote safely tied up behind Mitterrand and with the Socialist vote so far ahead of that of the Communists) Mitterrand was in an exceptionally strong position to appeal to disillusioned voters outside the camp of the Left. Mitterrand's alternative approach was based on his 110 propositions (which was drawn from the Socialist programme, *Projet Socialiste*, and the Common Programme) and was an attractive blend of Keynesian expansion, French-style public ownership and industrial intervention, and policies of redistributive social spending and social reform characteristic of Scandinavian Social Democracy but less well known in France. It is significant that, according to a Sofres post-election poll, most people thought that Giscard had lost because of unemployment and that Mitterrand had won because of his promise to bring about changes in French society.[7]

THE FRENCH SOCIALIST EXPERIMENT

After his victory, Mitterrand immediately dissolved the National Assembly and, in the ensuing parliamentary elections, helped the Socialists win an overall majority. The Socialist faction leaders were well represented in the new government. Pierre Mauroy became Prime Minister; Michel Rocard Minister of Planning; the left-wing Ceres leader Jean-Pierre Chèvènement, Minister for Research; the veteran Gaston Deferre, Minister of the Interior; Claude Cheyson, former EEC Commissioner, Foreign Minister; and Jacques Delors, Finance Minister. In order to keep faith with Communist voters and protect his trade union flank, Mitterrand also appointed four Communist Ministers.

The new Socialist Government quickly introduced a number of significant reforms. These covered social welfare, workers' rights, decentralisation and personal liberties. A new Ministry of National Solidarity, under Nicole Questiaux, was set up, social benefits for the less well off substantially increased and a wealth tax introduced (see Chapter 10 for a fuller discussion). The Auroux laws gave employees and trade unions strengthened rights, covering unfair dismissal, health and safety, information, representation and collective bargaining. The Deferre law reduced the powers of the prefect, increased the powers of local government, and established elected regional councils.[8] The Mitterrand Government also abolished the death penalty, ended the explusion of immigrants, got rid of the 'security' court and acted to control police harrassment.

However, Mitterrand's major priority was to deal with the economy. In line with the commitment to bring down unemployment and increase growth, the new Government took immediate steps to expand demand by increases in the minimum wage and social benefits (including family and housing allowances and old age pensions) which were paid for in part by deficit financing. It announced plans to create additional public service jobs, as well as special projects to assist youth unemployment. It also began to develop a number of measures designed to change the distribution of work: these included a reduction of the working week to 39 hours, and encouraging earlier retirement and the employment of young workers through the so-called 'solidarity' agreements between employers and unions (to which the Government made a financial contribution).

In the longer term, the Socialists hoped to improve the efficiency of the French economy through structural change, more investment and the adoption of new technology. The main structural initiative (foreshadowed in the Common Programme) was to take a number of major industrial firms into public ownership, including St Gobain (parachemicals and construction materials), Thomson (electronics), Rhône-Poulenc (mainly involved in chemicals), Pechiney and CEE (electrical). The armaments manufacturing sections of Dassault and Matra were nationalised, while the government took control of the two major companies in the steel industry. Together these companies had a workforce of about 760 000 or 15 to 16 per cent of industrial employment.[9] In addition, 36 banks and two financial companies were nationalised which meant that 85 to 90 per cent of banking activity was now publicly owned.

It should be noted that nationalisation was less of a political issue between Left and Right in France than in many other European countries. Even before the Socialist Government's measures, the public sector was more important in the French economy than in any other Western European country, with the exception of Austria. The state had always played a major dirigiste role in France and, as Mitterrand often pointed out, De Gaulle himself was in part responsible for the wave of postwar nationalisations which included, not only the public utilities, but famous industrial companies like Renault. The Socialists argued that the new nationalisation measures were needed to help basic industries to modernise and high technology industries to afford the necessary resources, while the virtually complete control of the banking sector was required to assist investment in long-term projects.

BLOWN OFF COURSE

In the short term the main question was whether the government's strategy of domestic reflation was going to be successful against a background of international recession. The interim plan of November 1981 had assumed a 3 per cent growth rate and 400 000 to 500 000 extra jobs in 1982–3, and, though the targets quickly proved too ambitious, there were some early signs that the Government's approach was working. In the second half of 1981, GDP grew at a rate of 2.3 per cent and, in 1982, at a time when the output of most other economies either stagnated or declined, the French economy expanded by 1.5 per cent. The rate of increase in unemployment slowed down considerably: whereas between September 1981 and September 1982 unemployment increased by 42.9 per cent in West Germany, by 36.7 per cent in the United States and by 12.3 per cent in the United Kingdom (where unemployment was over 3 million), in France unemployment grew by only 9.8 per cent. Between the summer of 1982 and the autumn of 1983 unemployment stabilised at about 2 million. From 1981 to 1983 200 000 extra jobs were created in the public sector, while the solidarity contracts freed 187 000 jobs through early retirement and job sharing. The Government was clearly taking its commitment to tackle unemployment extremely seriously.

There were also considerable improvements in the living standards of the less well off. In real terms, the minimum wage increased by 11 per cent between May 1981 and September 1982, while the minimum old age pension went up by 30 per cent. A million and a half old people were also exempted from local taxes, while 800 000 did not have to pay television licences. Between May 1981 and January 1983 family benefits increased considerably; the purchasing power of the 2 700 000 families with two children increased by 40 per cent. These were all worthwhile social advances.

But in the summer of 1982 came the first major setback to the

French Socialist strategy. The Government's approach was threatened in three interrelated areas – inflation, the balance of payments and speculation against the franc. During 1981 and the first half of 1982, the Government succeeded in stabilising the inflation rate. But at a time when prices in other industrial countries were beginning to fall, it remained higher than either the OECD average or the EEC average and two and a half times higher than West Germany, France's main competitor.

At the beginning of 1982, both the Finance Minister, Jacques Delors, and the Budget Minister, Laurent Fabius, warned that inflation would start rising again either if the budget deficit was allowed to get out of control (though, at 3 per cent of GDP, it was still lower than most other comparable countries) or if a wage/price spiral developed. They also pointed out that a rate of inflation seriously out of line with France's competitors could have a harmful impact on the balance of payments and choke off economic expansion.

In the last year of Giscard's Presidency, in part as a result of the increase in oil prices, the balance of payments was in considerable deficit. The Socialist Government hoped to improve the position gradually by increasing exports and by improving the competitiveness of French industry. Though there was a 3 per cent devaluation of the franc (and a 5 per cent revaluation of the mark) in the autumn of 1981, both Mitterrand and Mauroy believed that a bigger devaluation was inconsistent with French membership of the European Monetary System. There was also considerable discussion of the need to 'recapture' the domestic market, but formal import controls, except on a temporary basis, appeared to be ruled out by membership of the EEC and GATT.

In the summer of 1982, it became clear that the continuing world recession was undermining the attempt to improve the balance of payments. The Socialist Government had assumed a pick-up in the world economy by the end of the year. But the deflationary policies of the American, West German and British Governments meant that there was either declining or stagnant output in these economies. The differential growth rate, combined with the higher French inflation rate, made it that much harder to increase French exports or recapture the home market. So pressure increased against the franc.

In June 1982 the Government announced a devaluation of 10

per cent against the mark. Action was also taken to bring down the rate of inflation by containing the budget deficit to 3 per cent of GDP and, more significantly, by the introduction of a four months' prices and wages freeze. Under the impact of the freeze, price increases fell to 6–7 per cent during the last half of 1982. In the last three months of 1982, there was also some improvement in exports. At the same time, the social gains of the first year were preserved. Throughout the second half of 1982 and during the first few months of 1983 the Mitterrand Government attempted, with considerable determination and no little skill, to preserve as much of its strategy as possible against a very unfavourable international economic environment.

However, in March 1983, the Socialists were forced by renewed pressure on the franc to give up their attempt to expand against the trend. The franc was devalued again (this time by 7.6 per cent against the mark), taxes and social contributions were increased, public spending was squeezed, and monetary policy was tightened. As a consequence of this shift in policy, the year on year inflation rate dropped below 10 per cent, and between 1982 and 1983 the trade deficit was halved. But the French economy grew more slowly in 1983 than the OECD average (0.7 per cent against 2.4 per cent) and from the autumn of 1983 unemployment began to rise by nearly 50 000 a month.[10] The French Socialist experiment of 'reflation in one country' had failed.

THE POLITICS OF AUSTERITY

At the European elections of June 1984 the Left did very badly. The total Left vote was only 39 per cent, of which the Socialists had 22 per cent and the Communists 11 per cent. A month later, President Mitterrand made the youthful Laurent Fabius his new Prime Minister in place of Pierre Mauroy and the four Communist Ministers left the Government. The administration also dropped the Bill to increase state control over the private school sector which had roused considerable controversy, particularly amongst Catholics, and the Minister for Education, Alain Savary, was replaced by Jean Pierre Chèvènement. In September the new Finance Minister, Pierre Bérégovoy, introduced a budget which confirmed the Government's change of direction.

Taxation was marginally reduced, while public spending was squeezed. The budget's fiscal impact was broadly neutral: the Government was relying on an increase in exports to stimulate growth, while unemployment, which was expected to continue to rise, was to be tackled by a series of special programmes. The control of inflation, mainly through incomes policy, and the reduction of the balance of payments had become the main priorities. By the end of 1984, inflation was down to 6.5 per cent and it fell to below 5 per cent by the end of 1985, while the trade deficit narrowed considerably. Unemployment rose to 10 per cent in 1985 but was still well below the UK level. In place of Keynesian expansion, the Socialists were now preaching the virtues of austerity, albeit tempered by the notion of fairness and the need to restrain the growth of unemployment.

The major political task now facing the Socialists was to avoid a crushing defeat at the 1986 parliamentary elections and, in particular, a defeat which would lead to a disastrous constitutional clash between a Socialist President and a Right-wing dominated Assembly. The difficulties facing the PS were underlined by the results of the cantonal elections in March 1985. Although the Socialist share of the vote was an improvement on their poor performance at the European elections, the UDF and the Gaullist votes together came close to obtaining a majority.

In April 1985 the Government announced that it was going to introduce proportional representation for National Assembly elections. It was certainly the case that the commitment to proportional representation was one of Mitterrand's 110 propositions. But the Right claimed that the timing of its introduction showed that it was mainly a response to almost certain electoral defeat under the old system. Rocard, whom Mitterrand had kept in second ranking positions despite his popularity, took the opportunity to resign from the government over the issue. Even so, Mitterrand and his Prime Minister, Fabius, believed that proportional representation offered the Socialists an opportunity of building a new majority which would be based, not on the old and now discredited 'union of the Left', but on a strong Socialist party, possibly allying itself with Centrist groups.

In July 1985 the sinking of the 'Rainbow Warrior' in Auckland harbour, New Zealand, and the clumsy attempt to conceal French secret service involvement led to the resignation of Charles Hernu, the Defence Minister and a close associate of

Mitterrand. It also dealt a severe blow to the Government's efforts to establish itself as a competent government.

However, at its Toulouse Congress in October 1985 the party pulled itself together. The Congress was billed as a clash between Rocard (who had the backing of nearly 30 per cent of party activists for his minority motion) and the mainstream supporters of Mitterrand, as well as a struggle for the succession. In fact, there was an impressive show of unity; the leadership sought to combine the electoral popularity of Michel Rocard with the command over the party of Lionel Jospin and the prime ministerial competence of Fabius for the good of the party. In calling for a strong Socialist performance at the 1986 elections, Fabius underlined the new assurance of the Socialists: 'We have abandoned the culture of opposition', he said, 'and absorbed the culture of government.'

In the event, the Socialists, inspired by Mitterrand's effective television performances, fought a strong campaign, centred around their success in strengthening the economy, their introduction of beneficial social reforms and the overall competence of their government. The result exceeded their initial expectations. The Socialists and their allies received over 32 per cent of the vote and remained the largest single party in parliament. However, the poor performance of the Communists, whose vote fell below 10 per cent, meant that the combined Left vote was only 44 per cent.

The Right, even without the support of the National Front (which won nearly 10 per cent), had a narrow majority in the National Assembly and Mitterrand, therefore, called on Chirac, the RPR leader, to form a government. For the first time in the Fifth Republic, the Presidency and the office of Prime Minister were held by politicians from opposing parties. It remains to be seen how "cohabitation" between Left and Right will work, whether it will last until the 1988 Presidential elections, and whether it will be the Socialists or the Right who will benefit the most from it.

CONCLUSION

During the recession, the French Socialists achieved virtual supremacy on the left, and also proved that, despite having been out of power for more than twenty years they could provide competent and compassionate government. Their initial strategy of 'reflation in one country' did not succeed. This was, in part, because of errors of judgement, especially the failure to devalue by an amount sufficient to give the French economy an initial boost and also the delay in reaching a satisfactory arrangement on prices and incomes. However, it could be argued that, given the contractionary policies being adopted by France's neighbours (including the West German Government), the Socialist programme was, in any case, too ambitious. In an open and interdependent trading system, a boost to French internal demand in 1981 was almost certain to lead to a growth in imports, to balance of payments difficulties, and to pressure on the franc.

In the restrictive world of the 1980s, the French Socialists found that they did not have the room to manoeuvre which they initially supposed. Even so, their reforms brought a long overdue measure of social justice and fairness to France, while the policy of austerity, adopted in early 1983, reduced inflation below 5 per cent and brought down the balance of payments deficit without a massive increase in unemployment. In the circumstances, the record of the French Socialists was a creditable one.

5   The British Labour Party: Decline and Recovery

The Labour party, which was in power from 1974 to 1979, did its best to cope with the impact of the recession on the weakened British economy. But its mildly expansionary policy was brought to a halt in 1976, and, after a period from 1977 to 1978 in which it appeared to have achieved a measure of balance in the economy its Government was undermined by the 'winter of discontent' of 1978–9. In opposition after the decisive defeat of 1979, its internal divisions made Labour seem irrelevant to a growing number of voters. Despite the high level of unemployment, it suffered a further and even more disastrous defeat in June 1983. However, after the election of a new leadership, the party staged a remarkable resurgence. This chapter examines how the Labour Government of 1974-9 responded to the world economic crisis, charts the decline of the British Labour party from 1979 to 1983, and assesses its recovery under Neil Kinnock.

A DISMAL INHERITANCE

The Labour party had not really expected to win the February 1974 election. Although the Tory Government's economic policy had been undermined by a combination of the oil price increase and the unbalanced expansion of 1972-3, the Conservative strategy of using the miners' strike to go to the electorate on the issue of government versus the trades unions seemed likely to pay political dividends. In the event, Edward Heath called the election a month too late, the Tories made mistakes during the election campaign, and Labour emerged as the biggest single party. Harold Wilson, the Labour leader, formed a minority government.

Faced by the oil shock, the incoming Chancellor, Denis Healey, took seriously the January 1974 agreement of the Ministers of Finance from the industrial world about sustaining the level of demand and accepting current account deficits. Until 1976 he tried to maintain activity in the British economy and keep up the level of employment. However, a number of factors were working against him.

In Chapter 2 we have already seen how other countries, particularly West Germany, Japan and the United States, gave priority to reducing inflation and balance of payments deficits and restrained their economies. This inevitably had an adverse effect on the British balance of payments. Imports, already swollen by the oil shock, rose, while there were less opportunities for British exporters. In 1974, the British current account deficit was the bigger than that of any other country; and, though the deficit was halved in 1975, it remained larger than that of any other country except Canada. Inevitably, the economy was dangerously exposed to speculation against the currency.

The other major difficulty was the level of inflation. Here Labour's inheritance from the Conservatives was a dismal one. The impact of the oil shock and commodity boom presented a severe enough problem. But these difficulties were compounded by the threshold agreements (contained in stage 3 of the Conservative Government's incomes policy), by the effect of the miners' dispute, and by trade union hostility to incomes policy. The purpose of the threshold agreements had been to dissuade unions from bargaining to protect themselves against future price increases by guaranteeing that beyond a certain threshold price increases would be automatically compensated for by wage increases. In a low inflation economy these agreements made sense but in the post-oil shock world they were bound to escalate prices still further. By October 1974 retail prices were actually 18 per cent higher than a year before and this triggered off more threshold agreements. Labour added an additional inflationary impulse. During the general election, the Labour party had promised to pay the striking miners the 30 per cent increase which they had demanded and in government Labour immediately fulfilled its pledge. This solved the miners' dispute but it also had a 'ripple' effect on other wage settlements and consequently on the price level. By mid-1975, the year-on-year inflation rate had reached 28 per cent, a much higher level than that of other Western economies.

The logical response for a socialist government seeking to combine full employment with a reduction in inflation would have been to introduce an incomes policy. The problem for the incoming Labour Government was that trade union hostility to incomes policy had built up under the previous Conservative administration. The best that could be done was to cobble together an agreement, the so-called 'social contract', by which, in return for the repeal of much of the legislation of the previous Conservative administration (including the Industrial Relations and Housing Finance Acts), increases in pensions and family allowances and the introduction of food subsidies, the trade unions agreed to restrict settlements to pay increases in line with increases in the cost of living. But as inflation was rising fast, such an agreement implied that the level of settlements would also rise accordingly, thus putting the official seal on a vicious wage/prices spiral.

The best chance for the first phase of the Healey policy came after the June 1975 EEC referendum when the Government (which had been reelected with a small majority in October 1974) felt confident enough to introduce an incomes policy. In July 1975 it reached an agreement with the TUC under which, during the next twelve months, no one would receive a wage increase of more than £6 a week, with no increases above £8 500 a year. The policy was backed by the full authority of the Government in the public sector and, in the private sector, by a ban on price increases caused by settlements above the £6 limit.

The £6 policy was remarkably successful. Increases in earnings were reduced from 27½ per cent in July 1975 to 14 per cent in July 1976. Inflation was halved. A further stage was introduced in July 1976 which brought the increase in earnings down to 9 per cent by July 1977, though, because the collapse of sterling in 1976, prices ran somewhat ahead of earnings during the 1976/77 stage.

THE IMF CRISIS

Ironically, it was at a time when inflation was falling and the balance of payments deficit improving that the collapse of international confidence in British economic policies took place. One explanation was that city and financial opinion believed that public spending was out of control. It was true that, as a consequence of public sector pay rises and the increases in subsidies and transfer payments, public expenditure had increased sharply from 40.5 per cent of GDP in 1973–4 to 45.5 per cent in 1974–5.[2] But nearly half of this increase was paid for by buoyant receipts and the remainder was financed outside the banking sector, so it could hardly be said, even by monetarists, to be inflationary. And, in any case, by February 1976, the Labour Government had already announced cutbacks in planned public spending increases. Even so, the City was not impressed. The 1976 confidence crisis was further sharpened by the view that the British Government wanted a fall in the exchange rate.

During the rest of 1976 the Labour Government fought a desperate rearguard action against international pressure. In June the Government negotiated a $5.3 billion swap arrangement with the US and European Central Banks. In July, the Chancellor announced a deflationary package of further expenditure cuts and payroll tax increases. In late September and October, minimum lending rate was raised. The new Prime Minister, James Callaghan, attempted to get the Americans and West German governments to provide a 'safety net' for the sterling balances. But it was to no avail. By late October the dollar exchange rate had fallen to $1.56, a fall of almost a quarter since the beginning of the year. The IMF had to be called in and demanded public spending plans cuts of £3 billion in 1977–8 and £4 billion in 1978–9.[3]

The IMF demands led to a prolonged debate inside the Labour Cabinet. The Foreign Secretary, Tony Crosland, argued that the IMF terms should be rejected and called for the introduction of import deposits, while the Energy Secretary, Tony Benn, proposed the imposition of stringent import and exchange controls. However, on 2 December, the Prime Minister supported the Chancellor, and the Cabinet agreed to accept further cuts.[4] The terms finally agreed with the IMF and announced on 15 December were for cuts in public spending of £1½ billion in 1977–8 and £2.2½ billion in 1978–9. In addition, the Chancellor wrote in his Letter of Intent to the IMF that 'an essential element of the government's strategy will be a continued and substantial reduction over the next few years in the share of the resources required for the public sector.'

In other words, the Healey strategy of attempting to maintain activity by boosting internal demand had been finally abandoned. The Labour Government had succumbed to the pressure of the international financial community and hardliners in the United States. Whether, given the strength of international opinion and the British balance of payments deficit, there was any real alternative is debatable. It is doubtful if either the Crosland or the Benn proposals could have prevented the financial crash and probable fall of the government which would have followed a refusal to accept the IMF terms, though it is just possible that if the Government had managed to spin out the negotiations until the new Carter administration (which was committed to economic expansion) had taken over the reins in the United States, humiliation might have been avoided.

In the event, the IMF-imposed constraints turned out to have been largely academic. As a consequence of the cash limits on public spending (introduced in 1975) the volume of public spending turned out to be 3½ per cent lower in 1976–7 than in 1975–6. So that at the time when the IMF (and the government) supposed the public sector borrowing requirement for 1976–7 to be 9 per cent of GDP, it had already fallen to 6½ per cent. In 1977–8, public expenditure was actually 6–7 per cent below the IMF level while the PSBR was 4 per cent of GDP rather than the 6 per cent which the IMF had demanded.[5] Even so, it was generally recognised that the Labour Government had suffered a severe psychological setback.

THE 'WINTER OF DISCONTENT' AND THE DEFEAT OF 1979

Ironically, the period directly following the IMF debacle, between the spring of 1977 and the autumn of 1978, was the high point of the Callaghan administration. Politically, the Government's parliamentary majority was secured by the pact with the Liberals which was agreed in March 1977. The Prime Minister, avuncular and reassuring, was popular with the voters. Inflation continued to fall, reaching 8 per cent in 1978. Helped by North Sea oil, by the 1976 currency depreciation and by growth in world trade, the balance of payments moved into surplus by the third quarter of 1977. GDP, boosted by the increase in exports, grew by one per cent in 1977 and by 4 per cent in 1978. In 1978 living standards increased substantially. Unemployment, which had peaked at 1 630 000 in August 1977, declined significantly during 1978. Throughout much of 1978 Labour ran neck and neck with the Tories in the opinion polls.

Any prospect of a Labour electoral victory was, however, undermined. In October 1978 James Callaghan decided to delay the election. The Liberals had announced that the pact with the Government would be terminated at the end of the 1977–8 session. Most Labour MPs favoured an October election. But Callaghan decided to postpone the election, apparently calculating that Labour would do better in 1979. He reckoned without the winter of 1978–9.

Labour's incomes policy, which had been supported by the unions in 1975–6 and 1976–7, did not have the official backing of the TUC in 1977–8. Even so, this third phase was relatively successful and the Cabinet believed that it would be possible to introduce a very tight fourth stage, based on a maximum increase of 5 per cent. It was wrong. A number of groups (including Ford car workers and lorry drivers) broke through the policy. In addition, there were a number of highly publicised public sector strikes, with the dead being left unburied, dirty sheets piling up at the hospitals, and rubbish spilling over in the streets. The breakdown of incomes policy and the disruptive disputes which followed undermined Labour's most effective political card – its claim to be able to get on with the trade unions better than the Conservatives – and so destroyed the party's credibility as an actual and potential government.[6]

On the 28th March 1979, the Government lost a confidence vote in the Commons and was forced into a general election at a time when the memory of the winter of discontent was still fresh. Not surprisingly, the Conservatives, under Mrs Thatcher, gained a decisive victory. They not only won seventy more seats than Labour but their lead of 6.9 per cent was considerably bigger than that of Harold Macmillan in 1959. Labour's share of the poll was its lowest since 1931, with many working-class voters, particularly amongst the skilled, deserting to the Tories.

THE ROAD TO 1983

If Labour had suffered a major setback in May 1979, its behaviour in opposition ensured an even more disastrous defeat at the June 1983 election. Admittedly, there were factors working in the Tories' favour. The victory of the British troops in the Falklands in the spring of 1982 gave a big boost to the Conservative Government and in particular to the Prime Minister, who gained a reputation for courage, decisiveness and determination. There was also a sharp decrease in inflation towards the end of Mrs Thatcher's first administration, from the high point of 21.9 per cent in May 1980 (for which the increases in indirect taxation in Sir Geoffrey Howe's first budget was in part responsible) to 3.7 per cent in May 1983. But the fall in inflation was largely achieved by an equally sharp fall in output and a very big increase in unemployment.[7]

The Thatcher Government, strongly influenced by monetarist theories, was committed to squeeze inflation out of the economy by cutting back the money supply and slashing public spending.[8] From Howe's first budget in 1979 through until the general election, the Tories continued to contract the economy, despite the impact on output (which in 1983 was still 3 per cent below the level of 1979) and unemployment (which increased by over 2 million between May 1979 and May 1983).

The most crucial mistake was the March 1981 budget. Although the economy was already plunging into deep recession during 1980–1, the Government actually tightened its fiscal stance while maintaining an overvalued pound. Indeed, under Mrs Thatcher the United Kingdom was the least Keynesian of all the major industrial countries, so it is hardly surprising that British output and employment suffered most.[9]

However, because of its internal divisions, the Labour party failed to benefit politically from the collapse in output and the growing unemployment. After the defeat of 1979, there was a prolonged struggle for power. An alliance of left-wing trade unionists, constituency activists, and a minority of Labour MPs led by Tony Benn, a former Cabinet Minister and candidate for the succession, successfully changed the party constitution. Under the new rules, the leader of the party was elected by an electoral college of MPs, trade unions and constituencies instead of by MPs alone, while Labour MPs were subject to reselection by their constituency parties. James Callaghan resigned as Leader of the Labour party following the 1980 party conference and Michael Foot, the candidate of the left, narrowly defeated Denis Healey for the leadership in the last purely parliamentary election for the party leader.

The immediate consequence of these reforms and the election of Michael Foot was the formation of a breakaway party, the Social Democratic party (SDP), at the beginning of 1981. The party was led by Roy Jenkins, former Labour Chancellor and the President of the European Commission, and three other Labour Cabinet Ministers, David Owen, Shirley Williams and William Rodgers, and was joined by other former Labour MPs, including some who were in danger of being deselected.[10]

The SDP rapidly negotiated an electoral pact with the Liberals, which was formalised under the banner of the Alliance. The bruising struggle for the deputy leadership of the Labour party, in which the incumbent, Denis Healey, narrowly beat the challenger, Tony Benn, greatly assisted the growth of this new third force in British politics. During 1981 the Alliance gained three spectacular by-election victories – at Croydon, Crosby and Hillhead.

Although the Falklands factor gave the Tories a big lead in the public opinion polls, it was always clear that the combination of a badly split Labour party and the emergence of a Liberal/SDP Alliance backed by about a quarter of the electorate would hand the Conservatives the election on a plate. In June 1983 Mrs Thatcher won a landslide victory by 144 seats. The Tory share of the vote was 1.5 per cent down on 1979 but the Labour vote fell by 9 per cent to 28 per cent – the sharpest fall by any party since the war and its lowest share of the poll since 1918. Labour was such a poor second that it ran only 2 per cent and a mere 680 000 votes ahead of the Alliance. At the June 1983 election, Labour was driven back to its bedrock support in its heartlands of the North of England, Scotland and Wales, in the big cities and among the unskilled working class. It lost its majority backing amongst the skilled workers and trade unionists, and failed even to carry a majority of the unemployed. The affluent, skilled and house-owning working class deserted the Labour party in droves.[11]

The causes of the catastrophe were fairly obvious.[12] The fact that Michael Foot was not able to convince even many Labour voters that he would be a good Prime Minister and that the party presented an image of a divided, quarrelling rabble was profoundly damaging to Labour's cause. It was also felt that there were too many activists whose first commitment was to the doctrines of Leon Trotsky rather than to the Labour party. Finally some of Labour's policies, particularly on defence and housing, were also factors in the defeat.

With respect to the economy, the majority of the electorate did not believe the Labour party when it said it could bring unemployment to one million within five years. This apparently over-ambitious claim undermined the credibility of Labour's expansionist approach. In any case, too many voters even among the unemployed (some of whom did not vote at all) did not believe that there was an alternative to the Thatcher strategy. Unemployment was blamed not on the Government but on other factors, particularly the world economic situation.

RECOVERY UNDER NEW LEADERSHIP

The catastrophic defeat of 1983 at least had the effect of bringing the Labour party to its senses. In October, at the Brighton conference, a new leader and deputy leader were elected. The leader, Neil Kinnock, was young, eloquent and charismatic, politically left of centre, but able to communicate with a wide spectrum of voters, particularly the young. The deputy leader, Roy Hattersley, who was a Cabinet Minister in the last Labour Government, also became Shadow Chancellor and developed a formidable case against the Government's economic policies.

Suddenly the Labour party, whom the political commentators were writing off as in terminal decline, had a future again. It was partly that the party seemed to have forged a new unity of purpose. The heirs of the political tradition of Bevan and Gaitskell, of Crosland and Foot, were working together for the common good. Equally important, the new leadership, backed by an effective Shadow Cabinet, presented a credible alternative government.

Labour's recovery was confirmed by the European elections in June 1974 when the party, with 36 per cent of the vote, ran a respectable second to the Tories, while the Alliance was a poor third. However, the bitter miners' strike which lasted over a year proved a setback to Labour popularity. The party's close links with the miners' union inevitably meant that it was associated with the controversial leadership of Arthur Scargill, the failure to hold a national ballot and the violence on the picket lines. But once the strike was over, Labour moved forward again. It did well in the 1985 county elections, nearly won the Brecon and Radnor by-election, and, for the first time, ran ahead of the Tories in the public opinion polls.

At the 1985 party conference in Bournemouth, Neil Kinnock asserted his leadership over the party. He chastised the Militant-led Liverpool Council for their 'impossibilist' tactics in opposition to the government's restrictive policies on local government expenditure. Despite a technical defeat on the issue of a Labour government retrospectively refunding the miners' union for money it had lost through fines imposed by the courts, he also won a moral victory over Arthur Scargill. For the first time for many years, Labour ended the party conference season ahead in the public opinion polls, while Neil Kinnock gained new backing amongst the voters. A continued lead in the polls over the next six months, an impressive victory in the Fulham by-election in April 1986 and major gains in the May local elections confirmed Labour's recovery.

CONCLUSION

The recession had seen a sharp decline in the fortunes of the Labour party. But by May 1986, Labour had staged a recovery from the 1979 and 1983 defeats and was mounting a challenge for power. However, there were still obstacles to overcome. Despite over 3 million unemployed and a gravely weakened manufacturing sector, the Conservatives still retained a significant level of support. The Tories were also encouraged by the division of the anti-Tory vote between Labour and the Liberal and Social Democratic parties which consistently received 25 per cent in the polls. Even so, there was considerable evidence that the issues were beginning to run against the Tories. In contrast to 1979 and 1983, large majorities believed that the preservation of essential services like health and education should come before tax cuts.[13] It was clear that, if Labour could convince voters that it could govern effectively, it would stand a good chance of turning out the Tories at the next election and providing the next government of the country.

6 The Spanish Socialists: Democracy and Modernisation

The election of a majority socialist government in October 1982 was not only an important milestone in the development of Spanish democracy but also a major event in the history of European socialism. In post-Franco Spain, the Spanish Socialists (PSOE) who had for so long existed only in exile or underground, quickly emerged as the major party of the Left and the main alternative to the Centre (UCD) Government of Adolfo Suarez. As the UCD disintegrated following the 1979 election, the PSOE, under the charismatic leadership of Felipe Gonzalez, became the dominant power in Spanish politics, and, after the victory of 1982, provided the young and fragile democracy with a firm, modernising, though economically cautious, government.

This chapter describes how the Spanish Socialists became the major party of the Left and the main opposition party, explains why they won the 1982 general election so overwhelmingly, and outlines the approach and policies of Spain's first majority socialist government, elected again in June 1986.

SUPREMACY ON THE LEFT

Although the Socialists had been much the largest left-wing party in the Second Republic, it was by no means certain that they would achieve supremacy on the Left in the new Spanish democracy of the 1970s. During the Franco period PSOE had been poorly led from outside Spain by a group of exiles. After the Second world war, this leadership pinned all its hopes on Western governments 'liberating' Spain from Franco but, once it became clear that this was not going to happen, it had no effective alternative strategy. Inside Spain, the party suffered severely from repression. Thousands of activists were imprisoned, including three consecutive executive committees. The consequence was that, as Spanish society began to change under the impact of economic growth, the Socialists were ill prepared, fragmented and disorganised.[1]

By contrast, the Communists (PCE), who had infiltrated the Francoist unions, were much better placed when worker and student movements started in the 1960s. Under the leadership of Santiago Carrillo, the PCE began to move towards a Eurocommunist stance, emphasising political pluralism, gradualist reforms and independence from Moscow.[2]

However, Socialist support survived in Asturias and the Basque country, and in the early 1970s an Andalusian group, led by Felipe Gonzalez, a young labour lawyer, re-established a national organisational network, working not only in traditional Socialist strongholds but also through the Union General de Trabajadores (UGT), the Socialist trade union. In 1974, a new leadership, representing groups inside Spain and supported by the Socialist International, took over the party. Felipe Gonzalez was elected General Secretary at the Suresnes Congress, while PSOE adopted a more credible strategy which was based on a gradual and cumulative 'conquest of parcels of freedom', through mass mobilisation, political pressure, and negotiations, with the aim of achieving a decisive 'democratic break'.[3]

The emergence of a new young Socialist leadership could not have come at a more opportune time. The assassination in December 1973 of Admiral Carrero Blanco, Prime Minister and Franco's closest ally, the serious deterioration of Franco's health during 1974, and, even more significant, the growing industrial unrest, were all signs that the days of the dictatorship were numbered. After Franco's death in November 1975, the new Head of State King Juan Carlos, confirmed Franco's Prime Minister, Carlos Arias Navarro, in power and an unsuccessful attempt was made until July 1976 to fashion a compromise between Francoism and democracy. However, the democratic parties gained the initiative and in the Spring of 1976 an alliance (Coordinacion Democratica) of the main parties, including the Socialists and the Communists, agreed to press for an immediate transition to full democracy. In July 1976, Juan Carlos appointed Adolfo Suarez, a young Francoist apparatchik, with instructions to establish a democratic system.[4] Within a year, strongly supported by the Socialists and other democratic parties, he dismantled much of Franco's state, successfully legalised political parties, including the Communists, legitimised the trade unions, and presided over the first democratic elections since 1936.

In the elections of June 1977, PSOE firmly established itself as the major party of the left, and the main opposition to Suarez. The Socialist share of the vote, 29.9 per cent, was much larger than the Communists' meagre 9 per cent, and only 5 per cent behind Suarez's newly created party, the Union of the Democratic Centre (UCD). The result was a personal triumph for Gonzalez, who had fought an energetic and attractive campaign, emphasising his youth and the need for Spain to become a modern, welfare democracy. It was also a moving tribute to the strength of the Socialist tradition (what Jose Maria Maravall has called 'political memory') that those families, communities and areas which voted Socialist before Franco, voted Socialist again as soon as they had the chance to do so.[5] It was as if the Franco period had never happened.

1977–79: BACKING DEMOCRACY

The period between the June 1977 and March 1979 elections was a time of consolidation for the socialists. The PSOE strategy was a delicate one. On the one hand, it had to establish itself as a potential party of government – the *alternativa de poder*. This implied building up Socialist strength at party level, in the trade unions, and in local government. Here the Socialists had considerable success. Party membership rose from 75 000 to nearly 200 000. By 1980 the socialist trade union, the UGT, had drawn level with the Communist-led Workers' Commissions (CCOO) in the factory electons. And in the first municipal elections, held in April 1979, the Socialists gained power in 1170 municipalities (including Madrid and Barcelona) – always an important staging post on the way to national power.

On the other hand, the fragile state of Spanish democracy, above all the potential threat from the army, meant that PSOE could not risk mounting an all-out attack on the Suarez Government. On the contrary, it had to give as much assistance to Suarez as possible in coping with the growing economic crisis, in drawing up a constitution and in resisting Basque terrorism.

Spanish governments had totally failed to mount a coherent

response to the consequences of the oil shock. By the third quarter of 1977, inflation was running at 37 per cent. There was also a mounting trade deficit and growing unemployment.[6] The situation was deteriorating so rapidly that in October of that year the Government persuaded the opposition parties, including PSOE, to sign a short-term emergency programme – the so-called Moncloa Pact.[7] The central features of the agreement were a 20 per cent wage ceiling, restrictions on credit and devaluation of the peseta. In return, the Government pledged itself to introduce a new and more progressive tax structure, reforms in the educational, health and social security systems, increased public investment, and greater trade union rights.

PSOE agreed to sign because something had to be done about the level of inflation. It also believed that the social reform part of the Moncloa agreement would benefit Spanish workers and their families. In a limited way, the Pact was a success. Inflation dropped to 16 per cent in 1978 and the balance of payments improved considerably. But the main credit went to the government, while it was the Socialists who were blamed when most of the social reforms were not implemented.

In December 1978, Spain adopted by referendum a modern constitution, drawn up by an all-party parliamentary committee (including the Socialists), which guaranteed parliamentary democracy, the right to a vote, freedom of association and regional autonomy. The role of the monarchy and the Catholic nature of Spain was also recognised. Although the approval of the constitution marked a major step forward for the new democracy, the need to create a consensus in its favour held back the development of the Socialists as an alternative to the UCD.

Another reason for giving support to the Government was the growth of Basque terrorism. Between 1976 and 1980, 236 people were killed by the Basque terrorist organisation (ETA). The threat to democracy was intensified by the reaction of some elements of the military and the Francoist ultra-right who strongly opposed the autonomy which the Basques and the Catalans demanded. The growth of regional nationalism and regional parties created problems not only for the Government but also for PSOE as well, as the party's main strongholds were in the Basque country, Catalonia and Andalusia.

The 1979 election, which Suarez called before the local elections, was something of a disappointment for the Socialists.[8] Although PSOE finished well ahead of the PCE (which received just under 11 per cent of the vote) and marginally increased its share to 30.8 per cent, the increase was more than accounted for by PSOE's amalgamation with the small Popular Socialist Party (PSP) led by Tierno Galvan who later became mayor of Madrid. Apart from the rise in the UCD vote to 35.5 per cent, the other main features of the 1979 election were the increase in abstentions and the growth of the nationalist and regional vote, mainly at the expense of the PSOE.

1979–82: THE WAY TO POWER

But, in the longer term, the Socialist defeat in 1979 proved to be merely a temporary check on their way to power. For, as the UCD disintegrated under the pressures of governing in the early 1980s, PSOE gathered strength and authority.

During 1979, there was an intense debate within PSOE on future strategy.[9] Shortly before the May party congress, Gonzalez declared that he would like to see the Marxist label dropped from its statement of aims (adopted in December 1976 when PSOE had defined itself as 'a class party and therefore a mass party, Marxist and democratic') on the grounds that it deterred non-Marxists from supporting the party. An amendment backing the leader's position was, however, defeated at the congress. Gonzalez then electrified the delegates, including the radical 'sector critico' who had voted against his strategy, by resigning as party leader.

At the extraordinary party congress in September, Gonzalez was triumphantly re-elected with 85 per cent of the vote. The Marxist tag was dropped from the party's self-description, though the party accepted Marxism 'as a non-dogmatic method'. The way was now open, in the view of Gonzalez and his supporters, to build up an electoral majority by attracting new support beyond PSOE's traditional base.

In its climb to power, PSOE received considerable assistance from the UCD. The UCD was always more a collection of tendencies, interests and personalities than a coherent political party. Its weakness was revealed in the three and a half years after its 1979 election victory, when the combination of severe

economic weakness, political failure and internecine wrangling
virtually destroyed the party.

The second oil shock hit an economy which had not yet
recovered from the impact of the first. Although in June 1981 an
agreement on prices, incomes and employment was reached
with the unions and employers, the Government made little
attempt to deal with underlying economic problems. By the end
of 1981, inflation was still running at nearly 15 per cent, unemployment had risen to 15 per cent, while the external deficit
remained large, even though output was stagnant. In addition,
little had been done to tackle the difficulties of the crisis-ridden
steel, shipbuilding and textile industries, or to sort out the
archaic management and widen the narrow tax base of the
public sector.[10]

After 1979 the UCD Government also failed to come to grips
with the other major Spanish problems – the regional question,
terrorism, coup conspiracies and the role of the army. Instead,
the various factions quarrelled fiercely and publicly over such
issues as tax reform, divorce legislation and education. One
commentator shrewdly remarked that it was when it became
necessary 'to move on from the tasks of elaborating the constitution to those of applying it. . .to move from general legal-
political principles to concrete political policies, that the political
incoherence of and the political differences within the UCD
came to the fore.'[11]

On 2 January 1981, Suarez, infuriated by his party's divisions
and unable to rely on a working parliamentary majority,
resigned. On the night of February 23, an attempted military
coup was only foiled by the courage of the King, who rallied the
army behind the new democracy. Even these traumatic events
could not save the UCD which, by the time of the 1982 elections,
had been reduced to a rump of Government Ministers, having
split in four directions.

In contrast, PSOE under Felipe Gonzalez, was able to project
itself to the Spanish electorate as a united party, eminently
capable of forming a cohesive government. In the country with
arguably the most pronounced inequalities in wealth and opportunities in Western Europe, the party put forward an alternative democratic socialist model as the way forward.[12] The main
points of the PSOE programme were a commitment to the
creation of 800 000 new jobs, more effective use of the public

sector, expansion of the inadequate social services structure, educational change, and democratic reform of the state machine, including devolution of power to the regions and local government and more accountability for the media, the civil service and the armed forces. In foreign affairs, the party was committed to joining the EEC, mainly to end Spanish isolation, and to a referendum on membership of NATO, which the Socialists then opposed.

If PSOE's 1982 programme was, in Spanish terms, a radical one, its impeccable democratic credentials were reassuring to less committed voters. By its insistence on a principled break with dictatorship in the immediate post-Franco era, by its willingness to cooperate with Suarez in setting up the democratic state, and by its calmness at the time of the attempted military coup in February 1981, the Socialists had established themselves as the foremost champions of democracy in Spain.

The result of the 1982 election was a resounding victory for Gonzalez and his party. PSOE almost doubled its number of voters (10 million as against 5.9 million in 1979) and seats (202 as against 118 in 1979) while its share of the poll went up from 30 to 48 per cent. The UCD's support almost totally collapsed: it won only 6.8 per cent of the vote and 12 seats. The right-wing Alianza Popular (AP), led by Manuel Fraga Iribarne, former Franco minister and ambassador to London emerged as the main opposition party with 26.6 per cent and 106 seats.

THE REALITIES OF GOVERNMENT

The new majority Socialist government (with Felipe Gonzalez as Prime Minister, Alfonso Guerra, the party's chief strategist as Deputy Minister, Fernando Moran as Foreign Minister and Miguel Boyer as Minister of the Economy and Finance) faced great problems. An overriding one was the defence of democracy against the small but still powerful elements in the armed forces which still hoped to undermine the system. During the election, an army plot to take over the country the day before polling day had been uncovered. Jose Maria Maravall, the new Education Minister, rightly commented that 'the protection of a fragile democracy from the threat of totalitarian subversion will be a difficult challenge for a long time to come.'[13]

Another major problem was the economic crisis. As in the 1930s, the coming of democracy had coincided with a world recession. The Government's inheritance from its predecessor was by any standards an unenviable one. This is how the OECD described the Spanish economy at the end of 1982:[14]

> Activity remained very weak; unemployment – at 17 per cent of the labour force – was high and rising; inflation was still hovering around 14 per cent – more than double the OECD average; and the current external deficit amounted to more than 2½ per cent of GDP accompanied by a substantial reduction in reserves. The financial position of the public sector had also become a matter of concern, with the general government deficit rising to 6 per cent of GDP reflecting both cyclical and structural factors. In spite of the progress made in earlier years in reducing structural problems, the economy was still suffering from widespread rigidities in the productive structure, the labour market and the financial system.

The Socialists had always realised that it would be difficult to reduce unemployment but had hoped that a combination of more effective public investment and world recovery would increase employment. However, despite their election pledge of creating 800 000 jobs over four years, the PSOE Government quickly decided that, given the unfavourable international environment and the weakness of the Spanish economy, any attempt at a French style 'reflation in one country' would inevitably fail. So they adopted an economic strategy of gradual adjustment, with the main emphasis on bringing down the rate of inflation and improving the balance of payments.

The Government therefore announced that public sector wages were to be kept below the national wage agreement, money supply was to be reduced by 3 per cent to 13 per cent and the peseta was to be devalued by 8 per cent against the dollar. As a consequence of these measures, the inflation rate fell by 2 per cent to 12.2 per cent, the external deficit was halved, and output, stimulated by a growth in exports, increased by about 2 per cent in 1983. But the increase in output was too small to prevent a rise in unemployment to nearly 18 per cent of the labour force.

During 1984, the Government maintained its cautiously restrictive policy. By the end of the year, inflation had been reduced to 9 per cent and the balance of payments brought into surplus. Increased exports assisted a 2.5 per cent growth of output. But once again this was not enough to stop a further rise in unemployment, which reached 20 per cent by December 1984.

However, the signing in October 1984 of the two-year Economic and Social Agreement (AES) by the Government, employers and the UGT heralded a new and marginally more expansionary phase of policy.[15] Under the AES agreement, wage increases for 1985 were to be kept to between 5.8½ per cent and 7.5 per cent, and reduced further in 1986. In return, the Government promised to implement pts (pesetas) 50 billion of public investment and introduce a pts 30 billion job creation programme, while a further pts 60 billion fund (to be financed equally by government, employment and incomes) was set up for retraining.

The Economy Minister, Miguel Boyer, felt confident enough to announce 'a change in economic policy in order to move on from a period of financial and industrial adjustment and strengthening to one of growth' In 1985, growth was expected to reach at least 3 per cent, though whether this would be enough to bring unemployment down significantly remained in doubt. The issue of unemployment was complicated by other factors, such as the growth of the 'black economy' which employed between 600 000 and 800 000 (hardly the jobs which PSOE had promised) and the plan to cut back jobs in the heavily overmanned state industries, particularly shipbuilding and steel, by over 70 000.

In July 1985, Boyer, who overreached himself in demanding the position of deputy Prime Minister, was forced to resign. However, the Prime Minister, whose own position remained unchallenged, appointed Boyer's close colleague, Carlos Solchaga, the former Minister of Industry, as his successor. Solchaga's 1986 budget demonstrated that there was to be little change in direction. Income tax was reduced for the lower paid and increased for the rich, but severe restraint on public spending was maintained. Although inflation was planned to fall from 8 per cent in 1985 to 7 per cent in 1986, unemployment was expected to rise still further.

In the July 1985 reshuffle, Gonzalez also replaced the Foreign Minister, Fernando Moran, by the technocrat Fernandez

Ordonez. Fernando Moran, who had negotiated Spain's entry into the EEC, unblocked the Gibralter issue and improved relations with France, was arguably the most successful Spanish Foreign Minister this century (see Chapter 11 for further discussion of foreign policy). But his ambivalent attitude towards membership of NATO, which Gonzalez had decided to recommend to the Spanish people, would have made him a liability in the forthcoming referendum.

The referendum on NATO membership, held on March 1986, produced a pro-NATO majority of 52.5 per cent on a 60 per cent turn out. The result, which surprised even government supporters, was a personal triumph for Felipe Gonzalez. In the campaign, he had had to justify both to his party and to the electorate his change of opinion since coming to power. An additional handicap was that the Alianza Popular leader, Fraga, had called on his supporters to abstain. The decisive factor, outweighing anti American and neutralist opinion, was the persuasiveness of the Prime Minister.

Under Gonzalez, the Government firmly established itself as a modernising, democratic administration. The Defence Minister, Narcis Serra, introduced farreaching reforms which brought the armed forces under political control, reduced their strength and concentrated their activities on external defence. The Socialists dealt sensitively and skilfully with regional issues, and even managed, following agreement with the French Government, to start to contain Basque terrorism. A serious attempt was made to make the Spanish bureaucracy more accountable. Appointments were to be made on merit, while the practice of civil servants holding two jobs was banned.

Significant educational reforms were also made: universities were given greater autonomy, while greater central control, and supervision was established in the mainly state-subsidised private schools. Although the Government's austerity policies ruled out substantial increases in social programmes (see Chapter 10 for a fuller discussion), efforts were made to widen the tax base and stop tax evasion. Legislation was also passed to ensure that pensions were properly funded, though this also entailed cuts in pension levels. Abortion was made easier. To sum up, the Socialists had introduced a number of important measures to assist in the modernisation of Spain.

CONCULSION

The PSOE Government's main achievement was to strengthen Spanish democracy and modernise its institutions. In the economic field, its approach was one of gradual adjustment, with the emphasis on reducing inflation and improving the balance of payments. The weakest point of the Government's record was the high level of unemployment. However, in the unfavourable circumstances of the 1980s, and with the underlying weaknesses of the Spanish economy, the performance of the first majority Socialist Government had been a highly creditable one. Above all, the Socialists have proved that they could govern firmly and resolutely. One commentator has concluded: 'This may sound an almost trite accomplishment, but in the context of the divisions caused by the civil war, the historic memory of the Left's conduct in power in the 1930s and the Socialists' inexperience prior to 1982, it is a very real one . . . . The Socialists are the undisputed masters of the political scene.'[16] The June 1986 election result confirmed their superiority.

7 The Swedish Social Democrats: The Model Revised

The fortunes of the Swedish Social Democrats during the recession were mixed, though they made a strong come back in the 1980s. Partly as a consequence of an uncertain response to the first oil shock, the party lost office in 1976 and did not regain it until 1982. However, although the so-called 'bourgeois' governments were in office for six years, they failed to stamp their authority on events. Full employment was preserved but the economy remained sluggish and exports lost market share. In 1982, the Social Democrats returned to power with an economic strategy based on a highly competitive exchange rate, growth through exports and public investment, and a Social Contract with the trade unions. In the 1985 elections, the party ran on its impressive achievements in increasing output and investment and in maintaining full employment and social expenditure, and was returned to power. This chapter considers the reasons for the setback to the Social Democrats in the 1970s, explains why the bourgeois governments in their turn failed, and explores the ingredients in the Social Democrats' revised approach in the 1980s.

THE SOCIAL DEMOCRATS FALTER

At the beginning of the 1970s, the traditional Swedish Social Democratic strategy (described in Chapter 1) which had been successful for so long came under challenge. First, radicals, including Social Democrats, began to question how far the party had been successful in achieving its redistributive goals. Secondly, the impact of the first oil shock and the manner in which the Social Government coped with it disturbed Sweden's economic equilibrium. Thirdly, for the first time the bourgeois

86

parties successfully united to form a non-socialist alternative to the Social Democrats.

On the issue of equality, studies published in the 1960s revealed that, despite Social Democratic achievements, considerable income inequalities and some degree of poverty still existed.[1] In addition, rapid technological change highlighted the necessity for increased rights for employees at their place of work. There was also growing disquiet over the concentration of industrial ownership into fewer and fewer hands. In 1969, the Social Democrats adopted the Alva Myrdal report which called for a greater emphasis on equality. The report accepted that 'while important advances have been achieved, we are nevertheless forced to acknowledge that great inequalities still exist'. It argued for a double strategy:

> It is a question of opposing the concentration of privileges and power in the hands of traditionally favoured groups. At the same time, special efforts must be made to achieve a lasting improvement and equalisation of conditions in favour of individuals and groups which have been left behind in various ways, the weakest members of society.[2]

In the 1970s, Social Democrat governments, under Olof Palme, embarked on an ambitious redistributive programme. Special help was given to the old, one-parent families, the low paid, immigrants and the disabled. A whole series of reforms, which had the effect of giving increased rights and powers to employees, were also introduced. These included legislation on health and safety and industrial democracy. Swedish trade unions were given the right to appoint representatives to sit on company boards and to negotiate, not just on wages, but on all types of issues. In 1976 the so-called Meidner Plan, which proposed the setting up of employee investment funds, was accepted by the Swedish TUC, the LO. According to this plan, 20 per cent of the profits of companies should go into a common fund to be administered by trade unions. Meidner argued that employee investment funds would help counteract the concentration of capital ownership which was so marked a feature of Swedish industry, reinforce the influence of employees at the workplace, and protect wage solidarity by ensuring that wage restraint in the more profitable companies did not lead to extra profits for a few.[3]

However, following the 1973 oil shock, Swedish economic conditions began to deteriorate. Given that oil imports supplied 70 per cent of her energy needs, the Swedish economy was bound to be unfavourably affected by the increase in oil prices. Unfortunately, these adverse effects were accentuated by other developments.

It was logical for the government to try to bridge the gap in demand (caused by the increase in oil prices) by counter-cyclical measures. As a consequence of this policy, the Swedish economy continued to expand and unemployment fell to 1.6 per cent in 1975, the lowest level for five years.[4] However what was also needed, if inflation was to be controlled and the balance of trade was not to deteriorate too drastically, was an effective incomes policy. But, in 1975, hourly earnings increased by 15 per cent, while total wage costs including employers' taxes rose by as much as 22 per cent. Inflation increased faster in Sweden than in many of her main competitor countries and Swedish exports lost market share. At the same time, the expansion of domestic demand sucked in imports with the result that, in 1976, the external current account deficit rose to 3¼ per cent of GDP, larger than that of many other OECD countries.[5]

So, as the 1976 election approached, the Social Democrats' strategy appeared to falter. Their traditional alliance with the trade unions had not prevented a self-defeating surge in wages and prices. The bourgeois parties, effectively united in an 'anti-socialist' bloc, were also able to exploit other themes harmful to the Social Democrats. As the economy slowed down and inflation increased, the level of taxation needed to finance Sweden's advanced welfare services became an important issue, not just for the professional classes, but also for the bulk of wage earners as well. In addition, the Centre Party campaigned successfully against the Social Democrats' nuclear power policy, which it portrayed as not only dangerous but also imposed by faceless bureaucrats at the top. The Meidner employee investment fund plan, though not officially supported by the Social Democrats, also came under attack. The 1976 election was a severe setback for the Social Democrats. The bourgeois parties, particularly the Centre Party, gained votes and seats and were able to form a government. The Social Democratic share of the vote fell to 42.7 per cent and for the first time in 44 years they were forced into opposition.

BOURGEOIS RULE 1976-82

Although the Swedish Social Democrats had at last been defeated, the bourgeois government, a coalition of the Centre party, the Liberals and the Conservatives, was to a great extent the prisoner of the political and social structures which the Social Democrats had established. A large majority of Swedes agreed that, at all costs, full employment and the extensive welfare services had to be preserved. The trade unions, so long an ally of Social Democratic governments, still retained their power. And the Social Democrats themselves, though unaccustomed to opposition, remained a strong, cohesive force. So the new government's freedom of manoeuvre was very much circumscribed.

The fact that the Government was an uneasy coalition of the three non-socialist parties also made it difficult for it to pursue a consistent line. In 1978, the three-party coalition broke up after failing to agree on Sweden's nuclear energy programme (the Prime Minister, Thorbjörn Fälldin, refused to compromise on the Centre Party's non-nuclear stand) and was replaced by a minority Liberal Government. although the Social Democrats narrowly failed (with 43.2 per cent of the vote) to win the 1979 election and another three-party coalition was formed, this second bourgeois administration also quickly ran into trouble.

Without a coherent economic strategy, each of the three non-socialist parties had pressed ahead with its favourite policies: the Liberals with their family-orientated social policies and foreign aid, the Centre party with environmental policies and subsidies to the farming and timber industries, and the Conservatives with their insistence on reducing the tax burden.[6] In addition, state subsidies to hard-pressed industries expanded fourfold between 1976 and 1979. Consequently, public spending grew in a largely uncoordinated way. In 1980, the coalition decided that priority should now be given to curbing the budget deficit, which in 1980 had climbed to more than 10 per cent of GDP.

However, in March 1981, the Conservatives, who were the biggest government party, left the coalition because they wanted immediate tax reductions, particularly to the better off, and bigger public spending cuts. A minority Centre/Liberal Coalition then formed a caretaker government, leaving the Social Democrat opposition in a very strong position. In the October

1982 general election the Social Democrats won 45.9 per cent of the vote and gained a working majority over the non-socialist parties.

THE RETURN OF THE SOCIAL DEMOCRATS: A THIRD WAY

Under the bourgeois governments, the Swedish economy had performed significantly worse than those of most other Western countries.[7] By 1982 industrial output had dropped back to the 1972-3 level, while between 1976 and 1982 the volume of industrial investment had fallen by 38 per cent. Since 1978, the current account had been in deficit (running between 2 and 4 per cent of GDP), while more ominously still Swedish exporters had been losing market share. The central government budget deficit was one of the highest in the OECD and between 1976 and 1982 inflation had averaged 10.5 per cent. The most favourable indicator in 1982 was the low 3.2 per cent unemployment level which, thanks mainly to the extensive job creation and training schemes (amounting to 3 per cent of the total budget), remained considerably below the OECD average of around 9 per cent.

In a speech in August 1982, Olof Palme, the Social Democrat leader, set out his party's economic strategy. On the one hand, he decisively rejected the Thatcherite policy favoured by Swedish Conservatives of big cuts in public spending because it would lead not only to increased unemployment but also to a waste of resources. It was also, as the British experience showed, very unlikely to be successful in bringing about an economic recovery. On the other hand, the classical Keynesian approach of expanding consumer demand (pioneered by Swedish Social Democrat governments in the 1930s) was also ruled out by the big balance of payments and budget deficits and the growing burden of foreign debt. So the Social Democrats proposed an alternative policy which they called a 'third way', designed to stimulate production, investment and employment.

The 1983/1984 Budget statement described this third way as follows:

> The new Swedish government has . . . chosen a third path, where the goal is to generate increased production and a de-

creased external deficit *at the same time* as employment is maintained and a foundation is laid for lower price increases . . .
the high priority which the government accords to the
employment goal is evident from . . . the assessment that in
the short run certain sacrifices will have to be made in the form
of decreased real income and lowered living standards . . . . The success of the strategy requires a judicious
combination of expansive and restrictive elements. Of central
importance here is the distinction – so vital for a small, open
economy – between domestic demand for Swedish and
imported products on the one hand and, on the other,
aggregate domestic and foreign demand for Swedish products.
In principle, the policy aims to restrain the former demand
while stimulating the latter.[8]

A key element in the Swedish approach was the immediate 16
per cent devaluation of the krona (more than most economic
commentators expected) which was accompanied by a temporary price freeze. The Finance Minister, Kjell-Olof Feldt,
argued that a large devaluation was necessary, both to arrest a
massive currency outflow and to give Swedish goods a real competitive edge. The 1983–4 Budget statement explained that
devaluation could 'help to resolve the underlying competitive
and structural problems, without capital utilisation falling and
unemployment rising still further'.[9] However, devaluation by
itself was not enough; if such a strategy was to be successful, it
needed to be accompanied by policies designed to prevent the
positive effects of devaluation being eroded by compensatory
wage demands and by other measures to promote investment
and employment.

To prevent incomes rising, the Social Democrat Government
relied heavily on the links between the party and the trade unions
which had been such an important part of Swedish Social
Democracy. The Government made it clear to both unions and
employers that employment must be given priority over wage
increases. In return, the unions expected the Government to
preserve full employment and welfare services, as well as
ensuring that employees received some reward for their
restraint.

As part of its side of the bargain, the Government's main
short-term initiative to encourage investment and employment

was a £700 million public investment programme (or £4 billion if put in terms of the British GDP). This was concentrated in the housing, roads, railways, power and energy insulation sectors and was designed to create over 40 000 new jobs, as well as stimulating investment more generally. In addition, two substantial extra manpower and training programmes were announced to help keep unemployment down.

The already substantial budget deficit, as well as the Government's strategy of helping the export sector, ruled out any major increases in social spending. However, the Government was determined that there should be a fair distribution of sacrifice. Four election promises were quickly implemented: cancelling the so-called 'no benefit days' for those drawing sickness benefits, restoring unemployment insurance in full, reinstating the grant-in-aid scheme for municipal child-care facilities, and bringing back the previous system of indexing pensions and other benefits. Child allowances and food subsidies were also increased. To ensure that other groups as well as wage earners shared in any sacrifices that have to be made, taxes on wealth, inheritance and gifts were increased, while tax benefits to shareholders were either reduced or abolished.

To prevent devaluation merely being converted into higher profits, the Government immediately imposed an obligation for firms to deposit 20 per cent of profits in a non-interest account with the central bank to be used for investment: it also brought in a 20 per cent tax on dividends as a temporary form of profit-sharing. In January 1984 the Social Democrats introduced, after intensive consultation and debate, a more radical kind of profit-sharing – the controversial employee investment funds or 'fund socialism', as the opposition called it.

The Government set up five regional funds, financed by a percentage of company profits and, more significantly, by raising company contributions to the pension system by 0.2 per cent, and administered by a board a majority of whose members were trade union representatives. The main objective of the funds was to buy shares in Swedish companies up to a certain level.

The original arguments for the funds (counteracting the concentration of capital ownership, strengthening the influence of employees, and assisting wage restraint) had been widened to include the need for new investment. It has been calculated that investment in Swedish industry needed to be increased by 50 per cent. Employee investment funds building up at the rate of about £200 million a year (big money for Sweden) would quickly become the major source of new capital. In this way the Social Democrats hoped to provide a corrective solution not only to the concentration of power and capital but also to the industrial investment gap.

PROGRESS AND PROBLEMS

The Government did not promise any quick benefits from its policies. Instead, it emphasised the long-term nature of its approach. It insisted that economic policy had to be firm and consistent, giving employers and unions 'clear indications and lasting norms'.

However, the strategy proved remarkably successful.[10] In two years, exports rose by 18.5 per cent, while imports only increased by 6 per cent. Swedish exporters regained market share and the deficit on current account was virtually eliminated. Industrial production increased by 15 per cent from mid-1982 to the end of 1984 (compared with only 3 per cent in the rest of Western Europe) and industrial investment also rose dramatically. Employment increased both in the public and private sectors and unemployment fell to 2.9 per cent.

The most difficult task was to bring inflation down to the level of Sweden's competitors. The Social Democrat strategy implied restrictions on internal demand and on living standards over a number of years. It also assumed that the LO (the Swedish TUC) would retain the authority over its affiliates which had been so marked a characteristic of Swedish trade unionism. Here the support of the engineering union for separate rather than co-ordinated negotiations created difficulties, while there was considerably 'wage drift' at local level. During 1984 wages rose by 8–10 per cent and, by the end of the year, inflation was still between 7 and 8 per cent, double the 4 per cent target.

In February 1985, the Swedish employers concluded an agreement with the unions which was in line with the Government's aim of limiting total wage increases to 5 per cent. However, in May, public sector salaried employees came out on strike and the Prime Minister himself had to intervene to settle the dispute. The Government was also forced by deteriorating trade figures and an outflow of foreign capital to impose a credit squeeze and raise interest rates only four months before the general election.

Despite these discouraging setbacks, the Social Democrats fought a vigorous and effective election campaign. Palme concentrated his attack on the Thatcherite policies of the Swedish Conservatives and warned of the risk of rising unemployment, social conflict and urban riots, so characteristic of Mrs Thatcher's Britain. At the September 1985 elections, the Social Democrats lost seven seats and their share of the votes fell marginally from 45.9 per cent to 45 per cent but, as the bourgeois bloc failed to get an overall majority, the party was able, with the support of the Communists, to form a minority government. Although the Liberal share rose from 5.9 per cent to 14.3 per cent, the Conservative vote fell significantly, justifying Palme's claim to have defeated Swedish Thatcherism intellectually and at the polls. Then in 1986 the tragic assassination of Olof Palme in Stockholm on the night of 28 February had the effect of uniting the whole country behind Ingvar Carlsson, his Social Democrat successor as Prime Minister. In a difficult economic climate and against the odds, the Swedish Social Democrats succeeded in maintaining their hold on power.

CONCLUSION

The Swedish Social Democrats had shown that it was possible to preserve low unemployment and an advanced welfare state in the harsher economic environment of the 1980s. The combination of a planned and sufficiently big devaluation, a public investment package and extensive labour market measures enabled the Swedish economy to change course onto a higher growth path without sacrificing fundamental objectives. Whether these achievements could be maintained in the longer term would depend on the effectiveness of incomes policy in bringing inflation down to the level of Sweden's competitors. Even so, Olof Palme was right when he told the 1984 party conference that 'the Labour movement has shown that the economy can be turned round without dismantling the social system.'

8   The Austrian Socialists: The Miracle of the Recession

From 1970 onwards the Austrian Socialist party (SPOe) was the most successful Socialist party in Western Europe. Elected in 1970 as the biggest single party (with 48.4 per cent of the vote), the Socialists, led by Bruno Kreisky, won the next three general elections (1971, 1976 and 1979) with an overall majority – each time with more than 50 per cent of the vote. Even in 1983, when the SPOe lost support and was forced to form a coalition with the Freedom party (the FPOe), the Socialists still received 47.8 per cent of the votes cast and remained the biggest single party.

The major reason for their outstanding political record was that, under the Socialists, the Austrian economy consistently performed better than almost any other European economy. Despite being dependent on imported energy for two-thirds of its needs, Austria withstood the two oil shocks remarkably well. Her growth rate remained above and her unemployment and inflation levels well below the OECD average. Indeed the Austrian combination of low unemployment and low inflation was almost unique amongst Western European countries during the years of the recession.

This chapter describes the main elements in their economic strategy, analyses the underlying factors in their success, and considers how far the Austrian Socialist 'miracle' is sustainable.

THE KREISKY FACTOR AND 'AUSTRO-KEYNESIANISM'

Bruno Kreisky's Socialist party was a creative amalgam of the old and new.[1] The pre-war party, with its societies, book clubs, schools and shops, was a 'counter-culture', a society within the state, whose members gave it a greater loyalty than they were prepared to offer to the fragile Austrian republic. Something of this old tradition lived on. In 1983 the SPOe membership was over 700 000 or nearly 1 in 3 of Socialist voters. There were special organisations for children, old-age pensioners, women, trade unionists, families, the self-employed, tenants' associations, teachers and intellectuals. There were 70 000 'collectors' whose job it was to make a monthly visit to every member's home. There were five Socialist daily newspapers and an extensive educational network.

But, in contrast to its attitude to the First Republic, the SPOe was strongly committed to the survival of the Second Republic. The Socialists not only contributed to but benefited from this new approach to the state. Until 1966, a 'grand coalition' of the two main parties, the Socialists and the Peoples party (OVPe), carried out the postwar reconstruction of the country and negotiated the end of the four-power occupation. Under the system of *proporz*, each party acquired separate spheres of influence in the distribution of key jobs.[2] The SPOe traditionally claimed the Vice-Chancellorship, the Ministeries of the Interior, Justice, Social Affairs and Transport, as well as important posts in the civil service, nationalised industries and the banks. It was during this period that Austria's celebrated 'social partnership' was developed which helped provide the climate for cooperative industrial relations and incomes policies.

Bruno Kreisky, who was elected party chairman in 1967 a year after the breakdown of the grand coalition, at once set about making the SPOe Austria's majority party. A Jewish intellectual and former Foreign Minister who had spent the war years in Sweden, Kreisky was strongly influenced by Swedish socialism. In its 1958 *New Programme*, the SPOe had already broken with its Marxist past and made clear its commitment to democracy.[3] Kreisky now enlisted the help of over a thousand experts in putting forward well-argued policy alternatives to the OVPe on a number of issues, including economic strategy, education, housing, culture and transport. In 1970 and at subsequent elections, he successfully appealed beyond the SPOe's traditional working-class support to Catholics, liberals, salaried employees, professionals and even farmers. These 'Kreisky voters', who amounted to between 5 and 6 per cent of the electorate, were a vital part of the new Socialist majority.

The Kreisky governments of the 1970s combined social reform with a sustained commitment to Keynesian policies.

Public spending was increased significantly, with expenditure on education, health care and social services and benefits all increasing their share. Although the distribution of wealth and income remained substantially the same, special help was given to the poorest groups – the pensioners, the low paid, and the small farmers. Underpinning these social achievements (described more fully in Chapter 10) was the maintenance of full employment.

At a time when monetarist policies were sweeping all before them, the Socialists consistently pursued counter-cyclical policies – the so-called 'Austro-Keynesianism'. Instead of following the example of some other West European governments and deflating in the face of the oil price increases of the early 1970s, for three successive years the Government expanded the budget deficit to fill the demand gap created by the oil shock.[4] The result was that, despite an increase in the supply of labour, full employment was preserved. The increased deficit represented a deliberate decision by the Socialists to give highest priority to full employment. As Kreisky said during the 1979 election, 'I am less worried by the budget deficits than by the need for the state to create jobs where private industry fails.'[5]

Because of the need to prevent a deterioration in the balance of payments and too large an increase in the public sector deficit, the budgetary response to the second oil shock was more cautious. Even so, compensatory action was taken which helped keep unemployment below 4 per cent in 1982 (at a time when British unemployment had climbed to 13 per cent).[6]

PUBLIC OWNERSHIP AND SOCIAL PARTNERSHIP

Although budgetary policy was the main element in maintaining full employment, the role of the public sector was also important. Austria had the largest nationalised sector in Western Europe. The nationalisation acts of 1946 and 1947 (as much a product of the postwar situation and the four-power occupation as of ideology) added the extractive industries, including oil, practically the entire steel industry and most of the large enterprises in the field of machinery, chemicals and electrical equipment to the utilities (railways, gas, communications) already in public ownership.

Six out of the top ten firms were nationalised, while the three largest banks (which also had considerable industrial assets) were also in public hands. Despite considerable multinational invest-ment and an extensive small business section (both encouraged by government), the leading economic historian, Eduard März, has pointed out that 'the sheer volume of public ownership and investment made the presence of the state in the economy felt more ubiquitously than in countries with a purer form of capitalism.'[7]

In theory the nationalised industries were free to make their own decisions: in practice they had to take account of govern-ment economic policy. In addition many of the top managers were socialists sympathetic to government strategy. During the recession of the 1970s these industries played a key role in keeping up the level of investment and employment. It has been estimated, for example, that they reduced their labour force by only 3.3 per cent compared with a decrease of 7.6 per cent in industry as a whole between 1975 and 1979.[8]

To support their full employment strategy, the Austrian socialists also developed an effective counter-inflation policy. There were two main aspects to this: the hard currency exchange rate strategy and a genuinely voluntary incomes policy. The rationale behind the maintenance of a strong schilling (a policy devised by the then Finance Minister, Hannes Androsch) was that it protected Austria from importing other countries' inflation, fed through eventually into lower export prices and, by restrain-ing key elements in the cost of living, helped to influence collec-tive bargaining. But only a country which was also able to run a highly effective incomes policy could have successfully combined a strong currency strategy with low unemployment.

Austrian incomes policy was run by an unofficial body, the 'parity commission', which had been set up in 1957 with representatives of the trade unions, employers and government.[9] Although (or perhaps because) there were no rigid controls or quantitative guidelines over wages and prices, it was generally agreed by both 'social partners', including the trade unions, that the policy was extremely successful, particularly in the aftermath of the first oil shock. The level of wage agreements fell and infla-tion was reduced from 9.5 per cent in 1974 to 3.2 per cent in 1979 without even a temporary increase in unemployment and with real incomes increasing faster than in most other countries.

After the second oil shock, consumer prices rose by 6.4 per cent in 1980 and 6.8 per cent in 1981, but by the end of 1983 inflation had fallen back to under 4 per cent. The importance of this agreed approach to incomes was underlined in an OECD report: 'the incomes policy encompassed by the social partnership has played a key role in maintaining good cost and price trends . . . with inflation under control, the authorities have been able to pursue a more expansionary fiscal policy than would otherwise have been the case.'[10]

The key to the success of the Austrian counter-inflation policy was the support of the unions. Without the backing of the Austrian Federation of Trade Unions (OGB), one of the most powerful and centralised union movements in the Western world, it would simply not have been possible to operate an incomes policy. The OGB was able to speak with real authority on behalf of Austrian trade unions for two main reasons. First, 60 per cent of the labour force was organised into the 15 industrial unions which make up the Federation. Second, it was the OGB, not the individual unions, which held the strike funds and ratified wage agreements. In addition, trade unionists were represented in almost every aspect of Austrian life – in Parliament, chambers of labour, the party commission, the nationalised industries, the banks and in the Cabinet itself.

The link between the Socialists and the trade unions was as strong as in Britain, though it operated differently. There was no collective affiliation to the SPOe. However, the 'socialist fraction' dominated the OGB and was represented at the party conference. What was perhaps even more important for the success of a Socialist government was that the relationship between the political and trade union leadership was both intimate and sustained. Almost all the top leaders were Socialist MPs (Anton Benya, President of the OGB, was Speaker of Parliament), three trade union leaders were Cabinet Ministers while retaining their union jobs, and, during Kreisky's Chancellorship, Benya met the Austrian Chancellor every Monday afternoon to discuss the agenda for Tuesday's Cabinet meeting.

If the partnership with the unions was of great advantage, the social harmony which was such a feature of postwar Austrian life also worked in favour of a Socialist government. Though the SPOe had to respect the spirit and sometimes long-winded procedures of consensus (including extensive consultation on all legislation), the cohesion which was both its precondition and consequence undoubtedly gave legitimacy to the policies and actions of the Kreisky administration. The socialist 1979 electoral slogan, 'The Austrian way', effectively exploited both the Government's respect for Austria's postwar conventions and the backing which the Social Democrats were entitled to expect not just from their own supporters but from the electorate as a whole.

PRESERVING THE 'AUSTRIAN WAY'

After the Social Democrats' triumph in the 1979 election when they received over 51 per cent of the vote, the Austrian 'model' became a symbol of hope not only for fellow Social Democrats but for all those who insisted that there was a Keynesian alternative to monetarist policies. While the response to the second oil shock by other governments, including the SPD-led coalition in West Germany, was to squeeze their economies, Kreisky's Government continued to use fiscal measures counter-cyclically to compensate for the fall in demand, if somewhat more cautiously than after the first oil shock. Although the growth of output slowed down in the early 1980s, it was still above the OECD average, while inflation and unemployment were amongst the lowest in Western Europe.

Bruno Kreisky himself had become a towering figure, whose popularity at home and prestige abroad enabled him to play a role in international affairs far beyond what might have been expected of a leader of a small, neutral country. A prominent member of the Socialist International, he acted as a force for peace in East–West relations, as a spokesman in the North-South dialogue, and even as a mediator in the search for a Middle Eastern settlement. Both as Austrian Chancellor and world statesman, Kreisky made a significant and creative contribution towards the solution of some of the great problems of his time – unemployment, world poverty, and nuclear disarmament.

However, in the April 1983 general election, the Socialists lost their overall majority (in part as a consequence of the emergence of two new environmentalist parties) and Kreisky, who had been in poor health for over a year, resigned. A coalition with the small Freedom party (FPOe) was negotiated, with the former SPOe

Vice-Chancellor and Education Minister, Dr Fred Sinowatz, as the new Chancellor. If the new Government lacked the charisma of the old and was rather more circumspect in its budgetary policy, it successfully maintained a low level of unemployment and inflation.

It was, however, far more difficult to run a coalition than a majority Socialist government. The Freedom party, supported mainly by the professional classes, was an uneasy amalgam of liberal and nationalist views. At the beginning of 1985, the Defence Minister, a Freedom party member, nearly brought down the Government when he publicly greeted a former war criminal on his return from an Italian gaol. There was also a growth in Green sentiment. In addition public conflict between two former Finance Ministers, Dr Hannes Androsh and Dr Herbert Salcher, as well as growing problems in the nationalised sector and highly publicised corruption scandals, increasingly undermined the government's credibility.

The climax came in June 1986, when, despite allegations about his involvement in war crimes, Dr Kurt Waldheim, the former UN Secretary General and People's Party candidate, was elected president. Dr Sinowatz at once resigned and was succeeded by the Finance Minister and former banker, Dr Franz Vronitzky. Dr Vronitzky's task was to win back Socialist support in time for the 1987 election. Politically the Austrian model, or at any rate its Socialist version, appeared under threat.

The Austrian 'model' has been criticised from two different standpoints. From the left has come the charge that Austrian socialism was too pragmatic. Certainly, despite the special assistance to the poorest groups and a low level of unemployment, the distribution of wealth remained much the same. It was also true that, although Austria was a federal state, the political system was relatively centralised: many of the key decisions were taken by the Chancellor and a few top leaders, including a handful of trade union leaders.

Even so, the SPOe could not be accused of being a party without a sense of direction. The 1978 programme set out very eloquently the party's commitment to freedom, social justice, solidarity and democracy. More tellingly, the party's record in power – its preservation of full employment, its expansion of social services and benefits, its attention to its party and working-class base, its respect for human rights, its concern for North–

South issues and world peace – was a direct refutation of the charge of political opportunism.

Right-wing critics doubted whether the Austrian model could continue to be successful. In particular, they criticised the size of the public sector deficit. It is possible that, in the longer term and in an economy which is running at a relatively high level of demand, there could be a danger of the 'crowding out' of private industrial investment. There may also be a case, if demand management is to continue to be effective, for some scaling down of the costs of servicing interest payments on the public debt. But the coalition government had already taken steps to trim the deficit as a percentage of GDP which is, in any case, somewhat below the average of the seven largest OECD countries.

Conservative commentators also questioned the competitiveness and productivity record of parts of Austrian industry, particularly the nationalised sector. It is certainly true that, as explained above, the Government deliberately maintained or increased employment in the nationalised industries and the public sector as part of its employment policies instead of expanding its labour market programmes which, in contrast to Sweden's, were quite modest. And, despite the largely successful efforts of the Government to attract new investment, more high technology firms and industries were needed. Even so there was an encouraging rise in exports as well as a healthy balance of payments.

CONCLUSION

The main problem for the socialist strategy in Austria was the difficulty for a small and open economy of maintaining over a prolonged period a higher level of demand and employment than in most other countries. Most commentators agree, however, that, given the system of social partnership, the Austrian economy still remained better placed than most others to continue to combine a low level of inflation with a low level of unemployment.

It certainly cannot be denied that the economic and social achievements of Austrian socialism in the recession years were highly impressive. Whatever the special Austrian factors, the way in which Socialist governments so effectively combined intelligent demand management and a highly effective incomes policy should be studied by everyone who seeks a viable alternative to monetarism.

Part III
Policies Compared

9 Economic Policies: Managing the Recession

This chapter analyses the economic policies of the six European Socialist parties in the recession. For a fair comparison, it concentrates on performance in office: there is nothing about the French and Spanish parties *before* they came to power in the early 1980s, or about the British Labour party and the German SPD *after* they lost power.

Although the twelve years after 1973 provide a unity for analytical purposes, 1979, which was not only the year of the second oil shock but also the year when the major economies (including the United States, West Germany, France and Britain after the Conservative victory) adopted highly deflationary policies, clearly represents a watershed. Between 1973 and 1979 it was possible for individual countries to pursue a relatively expansionary policy; after 1979 it became more difficult. As has already been discussed (see Chapter 2), world economic fashion moved decisively away from Keynesian policies in favour of restraining the money supply and cutting public spending, and it became that much harder for individual countries to go against the trend.

In the period before 1979, this chapter concentrates on three economies – the German, the Austrian and the British. After 1979, it considers the experience of the French, the Spanish and the Swedes.

1973–9: THREE MODELS COMPARED

The most successful of the major European economies in the period after the first oil shock was that of *West Germany* under a Social Democrat-led coalition. Inflation was quickly brought under control and growth resumed, although at a lower level than in the 1960s. Unemployment rose to over 4 per cent in 1975 but by 1979 it had been somewhat reduced to a little over 3 per cent.[1] Until 1979, the balance of payments, despite the high cost of imported oil, remained in surplus.

In weathering the recession, the West German economy had obvious advantages. The success of their exporters in the 1950s and 1960s had put the West Germans in a relatively good position to pay for the increased price of oil and sustain their balance of payments. This strength in world markets was reinforced by the support given by German trade unions to moderate wage increases.

In the short term, the West German economy was also well placed. In early 1973, well before the oil crisis, the Government had put a brake on expansion at a time when most of its competitors were still expanding theirs. As a result, by the end of 1973 inflation was already beginning to slow down, while the balance of payments had been strengthened by the continued growth of foreign orders for German goods and to levelling-off of imports.

Then instead of switching to immediate expansion in response to the oil shock, German economic policy remained relatively restricted during 1974. It was the Keynesian policies of other countries, allied to a lower German inflation rate, which boosted the German balance of payments, helped expand output and stabilised unemployment. As a consequence of the strength of the balance of payments and the success in controlling inflation, the Deutschmark floated upwards. Though this increased export prices, it also reduced the import bill and encouraged moderate wage demands, thus reinforcing Germany's domestic cost advantage.

If part of the German success in the 1970s was attributable both to the underlying strength of the economy and to the relatively restrictive economic stance of 1973 and 1974, the intelligent combination of policies employed by the Schmidt Government was also of great importance.

In marked contrast to later, more monetarist governments, the Schmidt administration's strategy in the year's before 1979 was not to secure a single objective (such as control over inflation) but to obtain the best possible mix of ouput, employment and price. And in order to achieve these objectives, the Government also used a mix of economic instruments, including fiscal measures, monetary controls and a 'social contract' with the trade unions.

The balance between different policy objectives and use of economic instruments varied. In 1973-4, when controlling inflation was still the priority, the Government was content to combine incomes policy and the 8 per cent money supply target announced by the Bundesbank at the end of 1974, which Chancellor Schmidt believed would be a useful extra guideline to employers and unions. Even so in 1974 the Government introduced a DM 5.7 billion package of public construction works to create extra jobs – a policy very much in the Keynesian tradition. In 1977 and 1978, when the main priority was to bring down unemployment and help boost the world economy, the Government introduced two substantial expansionary fiscal packages.

Schmidt, however, always argued that the cornerstone of the government's strategy was the relationship with the trade unions.[2] In return for protecting living standards and employment and preserving the social gains of the Brandt period, the unions consistently delivered on moderate wage increases. This de facto but voluntary incomes policy did much to maintain the competitiveness of German exports and the stability of the German economy at a time of great international uncertainty.

After the 1979 oil shock, the Schmidt Government was no longer able to preserve the same balance between objectives. This time the reduction of inflation and bringing the balance of payments into surplus were achieved at the expense of output and employment. The problem for Germany was that, in contrast to 1974-5, the main industrial countries deflated their economies, so there was not the opportunity for German exporters that there had been after the first oil shock. The ability of the Government to introduce counter-cyclical measures was also more circumscribed, particularly by the increasingly negative stance adopted by the junior coalition partners, the Free Democrats. But the failure to prevent unemployment rising and output falling after 1979 should not be allowed to obscure the success of the Social Democrat-led coalition in combining low inflation, a relatively low level of unemployment, expanding output and a strong balance of payments in the difficult years of the 1970s.

The most successful of the smaller European economies during the 1970s was that of *Austria*. In contrast to most other countries, Austria, under a Socialist government, managed to combine a low inflation rate with a low unemployment rate. The inflation rate, which had climbed to 9.5 per cent in 1974, had fallen to under 4 per cent by 1979, while throughout the 1970s unemployment never rose above 2 per cent.[3] Growth of output averaged over 4 per cent, a performance superior to that of west Germany. Although the balance of payments deficit reached 3.6 per cent of GNP in 1977, by 1979 it had been substantially reduced without a significant rise in unemployment. No wonder that commentators began to speak of the Austrian 'miracle'.[4]

Austria had few obvious economic advantages to assist her in overcoming the impact of the oil shock and world recession. It is true that the economy benefited from the dynamism associated with a rapid move of labour out of agriculture. But Austria imported two-thirds of its energy requirements and as a small country exporting 35 per cent of its GDP, was highly dependent on the world economy. And, unlike West Germany, in 1974 the country was still enjoying the largest boom in its history. So, on the surface, Austria was not in a strong position.

The key to Austria's success lay in the combination of skilful economic policies and the strong system of social partnership. In contrast to the West Germans in 1974–5, the Kreisky Government quickly and consistently used counter-cyclical budgeting measures to counteract the deflationary impact of the oil shock and the consequent recession in world trade. As a consequence, Austrian unemployment scarcely rose at all. And, in contrast to the Swedish Social Democrats in 1975–6, the Austrian Socialists determinedly and intelligently employed an unorthodox amalgam of an incomes policy and a strong currency strategy to bring down the rate of inflation. By 1978, the Austrian inflation rate was one of the three lowest in Western Europe.

There is no way that the Austrian Socialists could have achieved such remarkable results without the country's celebrated 'social partnership'. The bold budgetary strategy would have had disastrous consequences if it had not been accompanied by a tough anti-inflationary policy. The hard currency policy would have led to a loss of jobs in export industries if it had not been accompanied by a strict incomes policy. The reason the Socialists were able to combine so effectively counter-cyclical measures to protect jobs, a hard-currency policy to control imported inflation, and an incomes policy to ensure that the level of wage increases was brought down, was the support of the trade unions. The traditional habit of social partnership was reinforced by the political loyalty of the unions to the Socialist leadership.

The low levels of unemployment and inflation as well as the flexibility which the social partnership gave to her economic decision-makers put Austria in a far better position than most other countries to withstand the second oil shock. In the 1980s, the Socialists persisted with counter-cyclical policies, if somewhat more cautiously, in view of the balance of payments constraint and a budget deficit which, though below the average for the main OECD economies, was larger than at the end of the 1970s. Unemployment rose to some extent but even so was still way below the OECD average, while the inflation rate remained amongst the lowest in Europe.

The main problem for the Austrian Socialist strategy was the increasing difficulty for a small and open economy of maintaining over a prolonged period a higher level of demand and employment than other countries. Even so, these difficulties arose not from failure but from success. The truth is that, by the standards of the time, the Austrian economic performance was outstanding.

The performance of the *British* economy between the two oil shocks was mixed, though there were some undoubted achievements. Inflation increased much faster and rose higher than in West Germany or Austria, reaching 28 per cent by mid-1975, while the 1975 balance of payments deficit was one of the largest in the western world. Unemployment was slower to rise but by August 1977 had climbed to over 6 per cent. However, by mid-1978 the annual rate of inflation had fallen to 8 per cent, GDP was growing at over 3 per cent, the balance of payments was in surplus and unemployment was falling.

Britain had been badly placed to withstand the first oil shock. In the 1960s and early 1970s, her exporters, in contrast to the West Germans, had lost market share. These underlying problems were compounded by the ill-managed Conservative boom of 1972–3. By the end of 1973, inflation was already in double figures, the balance of payments was in substantial deficit, and growth in output had ground to a halt. In addition, the incoming Labour Government had to face up to the consequences of both the miners' strike and outgoing Prime Minister Edward Heath's policy of indexing wages to the cost of living. No wonder that the London Business School predicted that 1974 would be the worst year for the British economy since the war.[5]

The Labour Chancellor, Denis Healey, was a highly intelligent pragmatist who learnt how to run the British economy in the difficult years between 1974 and 1979 by trial and a certain amount of error. In the first phase (from 1974 to mid-1975) he attempted to maintain output and employment by fiscal measures and to restrain inflation without the support of a formal incomes policy. In the second phase (from mid-1975 to the end of 1976), incomes policy was added. Inflation fell by half and the balance of payments deficit was substantially reduced.

However, as we have seen earlier, the Government was forced by an international crisis of confidence in sterling to call in the IMF, which publicly and humiliatingly (and, as it turned out, unnecessarily) forced the Labour administration to cut public spending, even though unemployment was still rising. The policy of maintaining internal demand by fiscal measures had had to be officially abandoned (at least until the Government had repaid the IMF).

The third phase of the Healey policy (from the beginning of 1977 to September 1978) was the most effective. Its success was in part explained by the 1976 currency depreciation and the growth in world trade, which helped British exports. In addition, North Sea oil for the first time made a significant contribution to the balance of payments, though the big benefits to the economy did not come until 1979. The Healey policy Mark 3, in fact, bore a close resemblance to the West German strategy of 1974–5. Output and employment were boosted by exports, while internal costs were controlled by incomes policy, monetary targets and a strengthening in the value of the pound.

The backing given by the trade unions to the Labour administration was substantial. From 1975 onwards, they supported the Government's incomes policy. However, in contrast to the West German and Austrian unions, their support was conditional. The trade union rejection of the 5 per cent norm in the autumn of 1978 was not entirely because the unions considered it too restrictive, but because many trade union leaders and activists believed that incomes policy was a temporary crisis expedient, not one of the main instruments of modern economic management. But the importance of the trade unions to a Labour government both politically as well as economically was shown by the disastrous impact of the 'winter of discontent' of 1978-9 on Labour's credibility as a government. Without an effective incomes policy, the Labour Government no longer had a viable strategy for running the economy. It was not surprising that the British electorate should have turned to the Conservatives who promised a different way of running the economy.

POST-1979: THREE SOCIALIST RESPONSES

The 1979 oil shock was a turning point in the development of the world economy. The United States and the three major European countries responded by deflating their economies. The consequence was a prolonged international recession. Almost all the major OECD economies abandoned counter-cyclical Keynesian policies and concentrated on reducing inflation. At the beginning of the 1980s far more than in the 1970s, most countries seemed prepared to accept much lower levels of growth and much higher levels of unemployment. One implication of this new climate was that any government which wanted to go against the trend would find itself operating in a highly unfavourable environment.

The Socialist government, which came to power in *France* in the summer of 1981, was committed to expanding the French economy and bringing down unemployment. Initially, this policy of domestic reflation had some success. In the second half of 1981 as we have seen, GDP increased by 2.3 per cent and during 1982, when the output of most other economies was either stagnating or declining, the French economy grew by 1.5 per cent. In contrast to other countries, the increase in unemployment also slowed down considerably.

However, the Socialist strategy was undermined by a combination of an above-average inflation rate, a weak balance of payments, and heavy pressure against the franc. In June 1982, the Government devalued, introduced a temporary wages and prices freeze, and announced public spending cuts. In March 1983, after further speculation against the franc, the government's expansionary policy was finally abandoned. As a consequence of this shift in policy, inflation fell to below 7 per cent by the end of 1984 and to only 5 per cent by the end of 1985, and the balance of payments deficit almost disappeared. But growth dropped behind the OECD average and unemployment rose substantially, although it remained considerably below the level in Britain under Mrs Thatcher.

It has to be said that the Socialist inheritance from Giscard was almost as bad as that of Labour from Conservatives in 1974 or that of the Spanish Socialists in 1982. It is true that the French economy had strengths, including a thriving agricultural sector and dynamic companies with a powerful position in the world market. On the other hand, by the 1980s France was far more dependent on the world economy, while 80 per cent of her energy requirements were imported. And the Socialists had inherited an economy which was severely out of balance. Inflation had increased to 13 per cent, the balance of payments was in substantial deficit, and unemployment was 7.6 per cent and rising.

Despite the poor inheritance and the unfavourable international climate, there was logic to the French Socialist policy of expanding the economy by increasing the incomes of the low paid and those on social security – 'redistributive Keynesianism' as it has been called. The growth target of 3 per cent was a modest one, while the planned public sector deficit was not out of line with those of other countries. French policy-makers hoped that a world recovery would boost exports and assist growth. Mitterrand explained later, 'Everyone predicted the return of growth by the end of 1983. Honestly I lack the necessary knowledge to say they were wrong.'[6]

Even so, the reflation strategy lacked the support of effective balance of payments and counter-inflation policies. A government, which against the international trend and without taking corrective action, expanded an economy with both a balance of payments deficit and an above average inflation, was bound to run into trouble. With French prices rising twice as fast as German prices, a devaluation against the mark was inevitable. The only question was whether it was to be a forced devaluation in stages (in the event the franc was devalued three times in two years) on a once-for-all devaluation which actively assisted French recovery. It has been estimated that a big initial currency adjustment would have improved output by 1 per cent and created 120 000 jobs, while boosting exports by 3 per cent and the trade balance by 24 billion france.[7]

But if the benefits of devaluation were to be retained, it had also to be accompanied by a tight prices and incomes policy to restrain inflation. In practice, the Government wasted a year before introducing such a policy, by which time the tide was running strongly against the French experiment. So, although reflating against the background of international recession was bound to be a high-risk strategy, the French Socialists did not take soon enough the necessary accompanying measures which would have given such a policy a chance of success.

The *Spanish* Socialist Government, elected over a year later than the French administration, did not attempt a French-style reflation. Instead, it opted for a strategy which gave priority to bringing down inflation and reducing the budget and balance of payments deficits. By the end of 1985, inflation had been reduced from 14 per cent to 8 per cent, while the balance of payments was in surplus. But, although national output had increased by about 2 per cent a year, unemployment had risen from 15 per cent to 22 per cent.

The Socialists inherited an appallingly weak economy – with rising inflation, rising unemployment, a big balance of payments deficit, and a public sector deficit well above the OECD average. From 1974 to 1982, Spanish growth, which had been such a feature of the late 1950s and the 1960s, was significantly below the OECD average.[8] The economy also relied heavily on indus- trial sectors (such as steel, shipbilding and textiles) which were suffering from worldwide over capacity, and on tourism and remittances from abroad whose contribution declined substan- tially in the 1970s. No wonder that the OECD economic survey commented that the incoming government was faced with 'a dif- ficult task'.[9]

With the Spanish economy so seriously out of balance and with the fate of the French experiment only too obvious, Miguel Boyer, the Finance Minister, adopted a broadly neutral budgetary policy. Output was protected by an 8 per cent devaluation which boosted the export industries, while a combination of monetary controls and incomes policy helped reduce inflation. A start was also made in bringing some financial discipline into the chaotic management of the public sector and the nationalised indus- tries. Boyer maintained that it was not possible to stimulate output and bring down unemployment until the economy as a whole was in better balance.

It could be argued that there was little or nothing to distinguish the Socialist Government's strategy of 'gradual adjustment' from an orthodox conservative policy. Critics could certainly point to the continued rise in unemployment as powerful evidence against the Socialists. In the Government's defence, it has to be pointed out that the pursuit of a Keynesian policy in an economy which was so severely out of line with the rest of the OECD countries might quickly have led to an inflationary balance of payments and currency crisis. A cautious approach was at least an understandable response and had the merit of consistency.

In any case, there were two features of the Government's approach which were different. The first was the deliberate use of devaluation to maintain exports, output and employment. The second was the attempt to create a framework of 'social partnership' within which policy could be discussed and agreed. Under the Economic and Social Agreement of 1984, the Socialist trade unions agreed to moderate wage increases in return for a commitment that the Government would expand public investment and develop job creation and training programmes. It was this element of trade union participation which made it more likely that, as the Spanish economy was brought into line with the rest of Europe, there might be a change of emphasis towards giving a higher priority to reducing unemployment.

The *Swedish* Social Democrats, who returned to power in October 1982, were determined to protect employment and the extensive welfare services. But Social Democrat leaders had already decided that the previous Swedish Socialist policy of expanding consumer demand was ruled out by Sweden's internal and external debts. So the new government pursued an alternative strategy based on devaluation, a voluntary incomes policy, and a package of public investment and labour market measures.

The policy was remarkably successful. National output rose by 2.5 per cent in 1983, and 3 per cent in 1984. Industrial production increased by 15 per cent from mid-1982 to the end of 1984, while investment also went up. Exports rose by 18.5 per cent, while imports increased by only 6 per cent. Unemployment fell to just under 3 per cent.

The contrast with the record of the previous government was striking. The Social Democrats inherited an economy in which output was stagnant, investment declining, inflation well above the OECD average, the balance of payments in substantial deficit with Swedish exporters losing in market share, substantial foreign debts and a public sector deficit which was among the highest in the OECD area.[10] The only bright spot was a low level of unemployment (3.2 per cent), maintained in part by extensive job creation and training schemes.

The engine of growth was devaluation, designed to increase exports, raise output and investment and secure employment. It was a bold and decisive measure. The devaluation was high enough (16 per cent) to give Swedish exporters an edge. Because Sweden was a smaller country, the major industrial economies did not need to follow suit. This meant that the Swedish advantage in world markets was fully maintained. And, as the adjustment to the value of the krona was made in one step immediately the Government assumed office, the potential benefits to the economy were maximised.

But if the gains of devaluation were to be preserved and the benefits to the economy fully exploited, there had to be a temporary decline in real living standards. A strategy built on such assumptions was always bound to be difficult to achieve, particularly in a democracy with only a three-year electoral cycle. It could only be carried through with the support of the trade unions.

At the heart of the Social Democrat strategy was a revised contract with the unions. On the one hand, the Government would give employment and protection of social welfare top priority, and introduce a radical form of profit sharing in the employee investment funds. On the other hand, the unions would moderate wage increases. Here the Swedish Social Democrats were less successful. Both in 1984 and in 1985 overall wages increases were higher than the Government had planned. As a consequence, inflation did not fall as far and as fast as had been hoped. Future progress in expanding output and maintaining the low levels of unemployment would depend at least in part on success in reducing the level of wage settlements.

INDUSTRIAL POLICIES 1973–85: A VARIED PATTERN

Although all six Socialist governments intervened industrially, there was considerable variation in the extent of that intervention.

The Austrian and French Socialists intervened the most. The public sectors in Austria and France were the largest in Western Europe. During the recession, the Austrian Socialists effectively used the nationalised industries to keep up the level of investment and employment.[11] The incoming Socialist government in France greatly extended the nationalized sector (see chapter 5), hoping by so doing to improve the overall efficiency of French industry. In addition, the French Socialists actively supported intervention in the nuclear, aerospace and telecommunications fields in order to produce industries which could compete on the world markets. However, after 1983 the need to reduce deficits and increase profits led to rationalisation and job losses in the nationalised industries.[12]

At the other end of the spectrum was the approach of the Swedish Social Democrats. They had traditionally taken the view that, provided private industry continued to pay for the welfare state, it should be left to get on with the job. Ironically, it was the 'bourgeois' coalition government which during the 1970s extended public ownership in the shipbuilding and steel industries. In the 1980s, the Social Democrat Government saw devaluation as the main means of improving the competitiveness and profitability of Swedish industry. It cut back significantly on government subsidies to industry, including shipbuilding and textiles, and clothing. However, it also increased funds available for labour market policy.

In the 1970s, the Social Democrats in West Germany (which had a somewhat larger public sector than Sweden) adopted a more interventionist industrial policy. The Bad Godesburg philosophy of 'competition as far as possible, planning as far as necessary' was to some extent modified by the recession. Industrial assistance was given to those industries which, like coal mining, steel and shipbuilding, had been most adversely affected. But, in addition, Government support for research and development was increased. At first, this was directed towards the high technology industries but in 1979 aid was extended to small and medium-sized firms. There was also (see Chapter 3) a considerable expansion of labour market measures.

The Labour Government in Britain (which had a larger public sector than West Germany but smaller than France or Austria) nationalised the shipbuilding and aircraft industries. It was also forced to take a number of ailing companies, including British

Leyland, Alfred Herbert and ICL, into public ownership. But the main achievements of its industrial policy were the creation of the National Enterprise Board to act as a 'pace setter' in key parts of the economy, the setting up of tripartite sector working-parties under the auspices of the National Economic Development Council, and the successful selective investment incentives schemes.

In 1982 the Spanish Socialists inherited a top-heavy, inefficient public sector which, under Franco, had included mainly loss-making industries and companies. In addition, basic industries like steel, shipbuilding and textiles, were suffering from over-capacity and were losing money. The Government took into public ownership the Rumasa banking conglomerate, Spains's largest holding company. But it acted to prevent a major crash and, once the complicated affairs of Rumasa had been unravelled, proceeded to sell back a number of companies to the private sector. The Socialists also carried out a major rationalisation of the steel and shipbuilding sectors.

Given the big difference between the policies of, for example, the Austrian Socialists and Swedish Social Democrat Governments (which were arguably the most successful Socialist administrations during the recession), it is difficult to discern any general pattern about industrial intervention. However, though most Socialist governments found it necessary to assist ailing companies and industries for social reasons, few of them were prepared to continue subsidising indefinitely industries or companies running heavy losses, unless, as with the railways, these were essential services. During the recession, Socialists in Sweden, Spain, France and even Austria had to take action to rationalise loss-making activities. But the argument for aid for high technology companies and for research and development continued to be compelling, as was the case for regional and labour market policies.

CONCLUSION

Throughout the recession, Socialist governments tried to combine low levels of both inflation and unemployment by a mix of policy measures, which included Keynesian demand management, monetary control, exchange rate policy, industrial and labour market strategies, and incomes policy.

On the whole, they were more effective before 1979 than afterwards. Before 1979, the Social Democrats in West Germany and the Socialists in Austria were both outstandingly successful. After 1979, as the experiences of both the French and Spanish Socialists in their different ways demonstrated, the hostile world economic environment made it more difficult to pursue expansionary policies. However, the Swedish example showed that it was by no means impossible. The relative success of the French Socialists, even during the phase of austerity, in bringing down inflation without a massive increase in unemployment was an indication that, provided they were prepared to persevere with incomes policy, governments did not have to adopt restrictive fiscal policies.

In these ways, Socialist governments convincingly proved that, contrary to fashionable monetarist doctrines, there were alternative and less restrictive ways of running the economy.

10 Social Policies: Defending the Welfare State

In the recession years, the idea of social spending came under sustained attack. As might have been expected, Socialists continued to be the most convinced champions of social expenditure. This chapter describes how, in difficult circumstances, Socialist governments struggled to defend the welfare state. Their record was, on the whole, a creditable one.

THE WELFARE STATE UNDER ATTACK

As has been described earlier (see Chapters 2 and 5) the 1970s saw a resurgence of right-wing economic ideas. One powerful strand of the monetarist argument was that the share of public spending in the national economy ought to be reduced.[1] The case against public spending was in part economic. If public spending was financed by taxation, increases in taxes, it was asserted, would have a disincentive effect on work and savings and stifle enterprise and growth. If it was financed by borrowing, this would inevitably lead to an increase in the supply of money and consequently to a rise in inflation. As a further twist, there was the danger, it was argued, that high public spending would 'crowd out' the private sector by pre-empting finance and resources. Conservative politicians (such as Mrs Thatcher, President Reagan, Prime Minister Barre and Chancellor Kohl) claimed that if inflation was to be controlled and enterprise stimulated, then budgets had to be brought into balance by reducing public, and particularly social, expenditure.

There was little hard evidence to support their arguments, certainly in the simplistic form put forward by Conservative adherents. With respect to growth of output, countries like West Germany and Austria combined high levels of public spending with above-average growth rates. The connection between budget deficits and levels of inflation was also far more complex than monetarists believed. For example, although West Germany ran a large public sector deficit throughout the 1970s, the German inflation rate was one of the lowest in Europe. And, although in a full employment, high growth economy, it was possible for increases in public spending to be at the expense of private investment, at a time of economic recession, with high unemployment and idle resources, the danger of 'crowding out' was scarcely a real one.

In any case, for many right-wingers the economic arguments mostly provided a respectable modern dress for older ideological beliefs. The 'new' Conservatives were against most postwar developments, particularly those that were associated with Keynesian policies, government intervention and the welfare state.[2] They opposed the growth of government public spending and redistributive taxation as being wasteful, bureaucratic and authoritarian. In Britain, where the spread of monetarist ideas went furthest, the Conservative politician, Sir Keith Joseph, provided his own list of what he thought were evil developments – excessive government speading, high direct taxation, egalitarianism, excessive nationalisation, a politicised trade union movement associated with Luddite attitudes, and an 'anti-enterprise' culture; while in 1976 even Roy Jenkins, then Labour Home Secretary, warned (on the basis of the faulty Treasury figures) that it was not possible to push public spending significantly above 60 per cent of GDP and 'maintain the values of a plural society with adequate freedom of choice'.[3]

It was certainly true that public spending, and particularly social spending, expanded fast between 1960 and 1975. A survey of trends in social expenditure in OECD countries showed that social spending grew in that period by an average of 8.4 per cent in real terms, compared with an annual growth in national output of 4.6 per cent.[4] But the drive towards increased social spending came not, as has sometimes been suggested, from weak governments capitulating to interest groups, but from the desire of a mass electorate to ensure that they were able to obtain some of the things that the middle classes took for granted – a basic income in sickness and in health, in employment or temporarily out of it, and in old age, as well as access to essential services such as health and education. The growth in welfare programmes was 'to a large extent a response to a common anxiety of large numbers of the population seeking more security for themselves and their families, to go with their new-found affluence'.[5]

Contrary to the claims of right-wing propagandists, in the 1950s and 1960s public spending was financed out of growth and taxation. It was only in the mid-1970s, and then overwhelmingly as a result of recession, that sizeable public sector deficits began to occur. The very low or negative rates of growth in 1974 and 1975 increased public sector deficits and pushed up spending as a share of national output. Although, with growing unemployment and idle resources, it made sense for governments to run budget deficits, these deficits undoubtedly created financing problems – a point which international bankers were not slow to stress. As we have seen (see Chapter 2), a number of right-wing governments took a lead in slashing public spending, while socialist administrations in Britain and France were forced to cut back.

As a result, between 1975 and 1981 the average annual increase of social expenditure in OECD countries slowed down to 4.8 per cent, though it remained above the 2.6 per cent growth in output. The pattern of spending also changed. The average for the seven major OECD countries shows that the real rate of increase of spending on health fell from 9 per cent per annum between 1960 and 1975 to 3.4 per cent per annum between 1975 and 1981, while the rate of increase in educational expenditure decreased from 6.2 per cent to 1.4 per cent in real terms. But if there was a decline in numbers of pupils (which provided an argument for governments to cut back spending on schools), there were increasing numbers of old people. This increase and a rise in the real value of benefits meant that there was only a small fall in the rate of spending on pensions – from 8.2 per cent to 6.8 per cent. The share of pensions in total social expenditure increased substantially, while there was a decrease in education's share. Not surprisingly, with the growing army of unemployed, there was a rise in the share of spending on unemployment benefit.

It is against a background of world recession, problems of financing public spending programmes, and, above all, of sustained intellectual attack on the idea of public spending, that the record of Socialist governments in social welfare has to be considered.

THE BRITISH LABOUR AND THE FRENCH SOCIALIST EXPERIENCE: ENFORCED CUTS

Both the British Labour and the French Socialist Governments, after initially increasing social spending, significantly cut back on spending programmes.

In 1974–5, the British Labour Government increased social spending by 9 per cent in real terms, though the growth was much greater for transfer payments and public sector pay than it was for services. In 1974, retirement pensions were increased to £10 for a single person and £16 for a married couple (a rise of 14 per cent in real terms), while in early 1975 there were rises in family allowances. In addition, there were substantial increases in rent and rates subsidies and £500 million worth of food subsidies were introduced.

Joel Barnett, Chief Secretary to the Treasury throughout the Labour Government, subsequently commented that 'there can be little doubt that we planned far too high a level of public expenditure in the expectations of levels of growth that, in the event, never materialised'.[7] Without the growth, the share of public spending in GDP jumped from 41.1 per cent in 1973 to 46.9 per cent in 1975. However, the initial decision to increase spending was entirely understandable. As we have seen (see Chapter 5), the Labour Government took seriously the January 1974 agreement of world Finance Ministers to sustain international demand. If there was to be a coordinated attempt to maintain world activity, then it made economic sense for Britain to increase social spending. It should also be remembered that the Government had made specific commitments to increase pensions and other benefits both in its manifesto and in its agreement with the trade union movement.

But (see Chapter 2) other major countries gave priority to reducing inflation and cutting balance of payments deficits. By 1975, the British inflation rate and balance of payments deficit were seriously out of line with its main competitors. And, contrary to the forecast in March 1974, the public sector borrowing requirement (PSBR) had risen sharply from 6 per cent in 1973 – 4 to 9 per cent in 1974–5; there was increasing concern that, in certain respects, public spending was out of control. Although much of the criticism was wildly exaggerated, account was understandably taken of City opinion, so essential to the borrowing of the money needed to finance the budget deficits.

The April 1975 budget brought cuts in planned spending of £1 billion (falling mainly on defence, food subsidies, nationalised industries and captal programmes), cash limits on 75 per cent of public spending were introduced later that year, and in August 1975 a 'standstill' was announced for central government grants to local authorities for the following year. The February 1976 White Paper confirmed the Government's decision 'to stabilize the level of resources taken by expenditure programmes after 1976/77', while in July, in response to a sterling crisis, the Chancellor announced a further £1 billion cut in public expenditure. Then, as we have seen (Chapter 5), in the autumn of 1976 the IMF were called in and demanded, on the basis of an inaccurate forecast of the PSBR, reductions of £1.5 billion in 1977-8 and £2.25 billion in 1978-9.

Obviously, these cuts had a significant impact on public spending and on social programmes. The share of public spending in GDP declined from its high point of 46.9 per cent in 1975 to 43.5 per cent in 1979 (though it remained comfortably above the 1973 figure of 41.1 per cent). Comparing 1973-4 with 1978-9, there was a slight fall in the proportion of national resources going to education, while only in health and social security was there a major increase.

Much of the rise in spending on health was accounted for by pay changes and cost increases in 1974. Undoubtedly the main social achievement of the Labour Government was in the increased financial support for pensioners and for the family. Between October 1973 and November 1978, the value of retirement pensions increased by 20 per cent in real terms, while a new long-term pensions scheme was established in 1976. In addition, a system of child benefits payable to mothers was introduced, which by April 1979 represented a net transfer of £830 million for the support of children. A Fabian essayist summed up the social record of the Labour government as follows:'The Labour record had some promising beginnings but became more discreditable with time. On balance, there were more constructive changes for the future than might have been expected. The child benefit scheme and the new pension plan were useful beginnings.' He pointed out that the Government 'was able to temper the effects of the recession to some people who were out of the labour force completely', though, mainly because of increasing unemployment, it was not able to prevent an 'intensification of difficulty' for many families of working age.[8]

In 1981, the *French* Socialist Government's social policies were closely linked to its economic policies. Economic expansion was to be sustained and unemployment brought down by augmenting the purchasing power of those on social security and of the low paid – a strategy of 'redistributive Keynesianism'. In turn, economic growth would pay for the increase in social spending.

The new Government moved quickly to fulfil its campaign pledges on social policy. Family allowances were raised by 81 per cent for families with two children and by 49 per cent for those with three children. Old-age pensions were increased by 300 francs a month for a single person and 3700 francs for a couple, while plans to introduce voluntary retirement at 60 were announced. Housing allocations for the low paid were increased by 25 per cent in 1981, while health insurance benefits were made more widely available to part-time employees and the unemployed. In all, the purchasing power of social transfers rose by 4.5 per cent in 1981, and by 7.6 per cent in 1982 – sizeable increases which together with the 15 per cent increase in the minimum wage between May 1981 and December 1982 significantly improved the living standards of the poor, the aged and the lower paid.

As a consequence of these increases and other increases to help employment and investment, public spending grew by 11.4 per cent in volume during 1981 and 1982 and the budget deficit increased from 1.1 per cent in 1980 to 3 per cent in 1982 – still below that of West Germany. The position of the social security and social insurance funds, financed almost entirely by payroll taxes on employers and employees, also deteriorated considerably. Then, as has been described (Chapters 4 and 9), the combination of an above-average inflation rate, a widening balance of payments deficit and strong pressure against the franc forced a change of course in the summer of 1982.

In June, the franc was devalued against the mark, a wages and prices freeze was introduced and an 'austerity' plan was announced to cut public spending in 1982 by 20 billion francs and to limit the budget deficit to 3 per cent of GDP. Significantly the Minister for National Solidarity in charge of social security,

Nicole Questiaux, was replaced by Pierre Bérégovoy, Mitterrand's chief of staff at the Elysée. Further cuts in public spending were imposed in the 1983, 1984 and 1985 budgets.

Bérégovoy told the press that his first responsibility was to 'know how to count'[9] and proceeded to reduce drastically the social security fund deficits through increased charges for hospital care except for the very poor, reductions in the cover and duration of unemployment benefit, and additional taxes on alcohol and tobacco. Other savings in health spending were achieved by giving hospitals a yearly budget regardless of occupancy rates. Indeed, so successful was Bérégovoy in bringing social spending under control that he was rewarded by being appointed Minister of Finance in July 1984.

However, despite the abandonment of Keynesian expansion, the social gains of 1981 and 1982 were largely preserved. In addition, educational spending increased its share of GDP. So even if the policy of 'austerity' brought a halt to the increase in social spending and resulted in increasing unemployment, disadvantaged groups such as pensioners and poor families continued to benefit from a Socialist Government in France, as similar groups had benefited from a Labour Government in Britain from 1974-9.

SOCIAL SPENDING PRESERVED: THE GERMAN, SWEDISH AND AUSTRIAN RECORDS

Two Socialist governments, the SPD-led coalition in West Germany and the Social Democrats in Sweden, were able to preserve their social programmes, while the Austrian Socialists continued to develop their country's welfare state during the recession.

The Brandt administrations (1969-74) in *West Germany* had substantially increased social spending. Between 1960 and 1975, social expenditure increased by 7 per cent a year in real terms, with a faster rate of increase in the Brandt years. As we have seen (see Chapter 1), many social reforms were introduced, including increases in the value and coverage of pensions, in the value of family allowances, in the coverage of health provision, and in educational opportunities. By the end of the Brandt chancellorship, the Federal Republic had one of the most advanced systems of welfare in the world.

The achievement of Schmidt, Brandt's successor as Chancellor, was to preserve the social gains of Brandt in the difficult recession years. Between 1975 and 1981, the growth of social spending slowed down to an average of 2.4 per cent a year in real terms. Even so, in 1981 Germany's proportion of GDP devoted to social expenditure was still the highest (at 31.5 per cent) of the seven major OECD countries.[10]

In the 1976 election campaign, Schmidt stressed Social Democrat success in the social as well as the economic and political spheres in putting forward his claim that, under the SPD-led coalition, West Germany had become a model (*Modell Deutschland*) for Europe and the world:

> Our country owes its high position to our successful policy of rapprochement, to our exceptionally high economic performance capacity, to our tightly knit system of social security, to our policy of constant reforms – and to the fact that we have put into practice our intentions about promoting social solidarity and real freedom for the individual.

Certainly, there were a number of useful social reforms during his Chancellorship. These included the replacement of tax allowances by child benefits as well as payment for the first child (1975), a new declaration of social rights (1975), a massive extension of youth training (1976), university reform (1976) and a sex discrimination Act (1977).

However, the main social security issue during the Schmidt Chancellorship was not reform but a crisis in the funding of the state pensions scheme (which accounted for 40 per cent of total social spending). Like the French social security funds, the German scheme was based on the insurance principle and mainly financed by the contributions of those at work. With the increase in unemployment, there was inevitably a decline in the number of insured employees.

During the 1976 election campaign the Government announced that pensions would be raised by 10 per cent in July 1977, in line with wage increases. But following the election, lower growth and higher unemployment forecasts indicated that, if the announced pensions rise went ahead, the fund would face a deficit of DM 10 billion in 1977 alone. After a political storm which led to the replacement of Walter Arendt, the Federal

Minister of Labour and Social Affairs, the Government decided to introduce a number of economies to reduce the pensions fund deficit, including delaying the 1978 pension increase by six months. Then, in the dying months of the SPD-led coalition, cuts in social expenditure were also introduced, including smaller increases in child benefits and higher unemployment and health contributions.

Despite their modifications, it is fair to conclude that Schmidt was successful in protecting West Germany's advanced welfare state during the recession years. It was a fitting epitaph on his Chancellorship that the issue on which Schmidt chose to break up the SPD/FDP coalition was the call of the FDP Economics Minister, Count Otto Lambsdorf, for big cuts in social spending.

The strategy of the *Swedish* Social Democrat Government, elected in September 1982, was to concentrate resources on production, investment and employment. In order to reduce the very large budget deficit which it had inherited from the 'bourgeois' administrations, social spending had to be restrained. But the government totally rejected the Thatcherite solution of big cuts in social expenditure as a means of revitalising the economy. On the contrary, the Social Democrats saw a strong welfare system as providing one of the main props of a strong economy.

As we have seen (Chapter 1), Social Democrat governments in the 1950s and 1960s had developed the Swedish welfare state into the most advanced in the world. Further improvements, designed to benefit the most disadvantaged groups, were added by Social Democrat governments in the early 1970s. In 1975, social spending was nearly 30 per cent of GDP. Then, under the bourgeois administrations (1976–82), public spending grew rapidly and in a largely unplanned way. In contrast to practice under the Social Democrats, growth in spending was not matched either by growth in output or by taxation, so that by 1982 the budget deficit had risen to 13 per cent GDP.

It was this deficit which, combined with the large balance of payments deficit, the high level of foreign indebtedness, and an inflation rate above the OECD average, ruled out the possibility of a French-style Keynesian expansion, based on substantial increases in social spending. However, in the Social Democrats'

'third way' (including a substantial devaluation, a public investment programme, and a contract with the unions), social
priorities were maintained.

If wage earners had to take a substantial cut in real earnings
and if pensioners (benefiting from the most generous pension
scheme in the world) were not to be compensated for price
increases caused by devaluation, then the better off had to make
sacrifices. It was for this reason that the tax on wealth was
increased, tax benefits for shareholders reduced or abolished,
and profit sharing introduced. As we have seen earlier four
election promises to increase social benefits were also quickly
implemented. In addition child allowances and food subsidies
were increased.

At the party conference in September 1984, Olof Palme, Prime
Minister and party chairman, described his party's record in
these words:

> After two years, the labour movement has shown that the
> economy can be turned round without dismantling the social
> system. We refuse to accept new liberalism's recipe of higher
> unemployment and welfare cuts. . .Our aim is to restore full
> employment and maintain welfare services. Unemployment
> and welfare cuts increase divisiveness. Freedom lies in security
> of employment and welfare.

Palme was referring to two crucial points. Firstly, increased
growth in the Swedish economy by increasing the tax-take had
reduced the budget deficit *without* the need for cuts in services.
Second, the Swedish welfare system and low unemployment, far
from weakening the economy, had actually strengthened it.
Indeed, Kjell-Olof Feldt, the Social Democrat Finance Minister,
persuasively argued that modility and change were much easier
to achieve against a background of security of employment and
welfare than in a high unemployment, low welfare economy.[11]
One shrewdly summed up the Social Democrat position as
follows:

> The Social Democrats are trying to re-define the welfare state
> in a manner compatible with economic constraints; their
> economic recovery policies impose limits on their social
> welfare ambitions but, rather than viewing the welfare state as
> a luxury affordable only in the context of economic success,

they insist on its positive role in facilitating economic adaptation.[12]

During the recession, *Austrian* Socialist Governments continued to develop their social and welfare services, if at a marginally slower rate than before. Between 1960 and 1975, social spending increased at an average rate of 6.7 per cent per year, while from 1975 to 1981 it rose at an average rate of 5 per cent per year. By 1981 the share of social spending in GDP had climbed from 18 per cent in 1960 to nearly 28 per cent.

In Austria, social policy since 1945 had been within the sphere of the 'social partnership' system. On social welfare issues, the Austrian Federation of Trade Unions (OGB) has been extremely influential, so much so that it has been said that 'the guidelines for the social policy of the 1960s and 1970s were fixed at the OGB congresses of 1955 and 1959'.[13] From 1965, old age pensions were adjusted annually to increases in earnings. By 1966, the coverage of the health services was virtually comprehensive. Before that, in 1959, family support had been extended to cover the entire population. In 1962, the basic school organisation law was passed which made education primarily a federal responsibility and required a two-thirds majority of the National Council for any legislative change. All those were measures introduced by the grand coalition between the Socialists and the People's Party (OVP).

Ruling on their own, Socialist governments in the 1970s and early 1980s extended the welfare state in a number of significant ways. Full sick pay was extended to blue collar unions (1974) and four weeks paid holiday was introduced (1976).Family benefits were expanded to include a marriage payment (1972), a birth payment (1976), full school transport (1971), and payment for school books (1974). In 1978, as a result of a change from tax allowances to direct payments for children, family benefits increased considerably.

Between 1973 and 1980 spending on health and education increased on average by 13.7 per cent and by 12.9 per cent per annum respectively. Although the Socialists failed to win the necessary two-thirds majority to introduce comprehensive secondary education up to 14, pupil/teacher ratios fell sharply and a new university law was passed (1975) to make higher education more democratic. By any standards, this was an impressive record of reform – particularly during the recession.

However, the Socialists were fully aware of the precarious nature of their achievement. In their 1978 party programme they warned not only that the right-wing demand for a reduction in public expenditure would be at the expense of welfare and employment but also that welfare was threatened by 'economic crises'.[14] It was certainly the case that only their skilful management of the economy and the room for manoeuvre which was afforded by their alliance with the unions and by the strength of social partnership enabled the Socialists to preserve and, in some areas, extend the Austrian welfare state in the recession year.

THE SPANISH SOCIALISTS – A SPECIAL CASE

The position of the Spanish Socialists on social spending represents somewhat of a special case. Although the Franco regime had left Spanish welfare services considerably behind those of most West European countries, social spending had increased rapidly after Franco's death but without a matching increase in either output or in taxation. And, as was described in Chapter 6, the Socialist Government, elected in October 1982, inherited an economy severely out of balance, including a big balance of payments deficit, an inflation rate double the OECD average, as well as a large budget deficit. The Socialists were, therefore, badly placed to make substantial improvements in welfare.

Under Franco, the welfare state had not been developed as it had in the rest of Western Europe. The regime was just not 'geared to thinking in terms of major social expenditure'.[15] In 1975, when Franco died, social spending represented only 12 per cent of GDP, under half the average of EEC countries, social inequalities were far more pronounced, and the tax base was grossly inadequate.

With the coming of democracy, and especially after the Moncloa Pact in 1977, there was a major expansion of social spending. From 1977 to 1983 spending on social benefits as a whole grew by about 28 per cent, with expenditure on pensions increasing even faster. In real terms, average monthly pensions rose in value by approximately 4.5 per cent a year. However, given the appallingly low starting level, the value of the pension in 1983 was still only 70 per cent of the minimum wage. And, although there was a rise in the level of unemployment benefit, only 50 per cent of the unemployed received it.

Yet even though these improvements did not bring Spanish welfare services up to the average Western European standard, they were enough to strain the resources of the state. In part, this was because from 1974 onwards growth of output fell not only well below the level of the 1960s but also below the OECD average. In part, it was because of the inadequate tax base of the economy. In 1979 the percentage of tax income per capita was the lowest in Western Europe. And in part, it was because the burden of financing social security payments fell heavily on employers who, in 1983 contributed 45 per cent of total tax receipts – the highest proportion amongst OECD member countries.

However, the policies of the Socialists, designed to bring the Spanish economy into balance, ruled out substantial increases in social spending. As we have seen the Education Minister, Jose Maria Maravall introduced major educational reforms in both schools and universities. There were also significant job-creation programmes. Attempts were made to widen the tax base and stop tax evasion. But the most notable reform in the social security field was pensions legislation in 1985 which involved cuts in the average level of new pensions as well as a progressive extension of the qualifying contribution period.

The purpose of the legislation, which was fiercely opposed by the unions, was to reduce the rapidly increasing deficit of the pension fund, as well as to increase the level of central government contribution and provide a guarantee of inflation-proofing. In the Spain of the 1980s with its weakened economy and insecurely based welfare, the Socialist Government's priority was to ensure that social programmes were properly funded.

POLICIES FOR 'SOLIDARITY'

A characteristic feature of European Socialism during the recession was the commitment to 'solidarity' strategies. These centred around a compact with the trade unions and linked together economic, industrial, social and distributional policies. They were most fully developed in Austria, Sweden and West

Germany, to a lesser extent in Britain, and were weakest, though still significant, in France and Spain.

There were overwhelming advantages for Socialist governments in having the wholehearted support of the trade unions for their policies. In the post-oil shock world, there was no way that these governments could successfully harmonise the varied objectives of full employment, low inflation and high social spending without full trade union backing for restraint over wage increases. For their part, trade unions could only achieve their goals – real wage increases, job security, industrial democracy and social welfare gains for their members – in alliance with socialist governments. In the most developed systems of social partnership (as in Austria and Sweden) there was also a role for management. Employers recognised that full employment and welfare were essential objectives of the economic system in return for an acceptance by unions and government of the need for wage moderation, higher productivity and a reasonable return on capital, as a prerequisite for economic growth, full employment and social welfare.

The most formalised and structured system of solidarity was the *Austrian* social partnership. In an earlier chapter (see Chapter 8), we have seen how the social partnership institutions, created in the 1950s under the 'grand coalition', played such an important part in the success of the Austrian Socialists in the 1970s and 1980s. The chambers of labour and trade with their statutory rights of consultation, the policy commission with its sub-committees on prices, wages, and economic and social questions, and, above, all, the long-term involvement of the Austrian Federation of Trade Unions (OGB) with its power over its affiliates and comprehensive representation, enabled Socialist governments to combine a low level of inflation, low unemployment, a high investment rate and a high level of social spending throughout the recession.

One authority has shrewdly observed that the social partnership

is based on the recognition that consensus among major groupings. . .is a prerequisite for the smooth functioning of a modern industrial market economy. In particular it is recognized that if social policy aims (e.g. full employment and social welfare) are to be achieved then economic policy issues must be addressed. More generally, the interdependence of the economic and social is acknowledged and the relationship, including the trade-off between economic wage and social welfare, wage levels and inflation, inflation and unemployment, forms the basis of the general policy approach.[16]

However, it should be noted that, although social objectives, protection for the weakest groups, and a flourishing public sector were given top priority, the Austrian model was not primarily a redistributional one. It was significant that, despite the predominance of the Socialists in the recession years, Ministers continued to emphasise the need to increase the size of the cake (and pay for social spending that way) rather than to reallocate the portions within the cake.

The *Swedish* Social Democrats' approach put greater stress on distribution and 'fair shares'. As we have seen (see Chapter 1), Swedish trade unions in the 1950s and 1960s supported a voluntary incomes policy, higher productivity and an active manpower policy in order to secure full employment, an equitable share of national wealth and increased welfare. In the 1970s, Social Democrat governments gave additional emphasis both to support for democratic rights at work and to social spending on weaker groups such as the disabled. If the Swedish model seemed less adaptable than the Austrian approach in combining economic and social objectives in 1974–6, the successful strategy of the Social Democrats in the 1980s relied heavily on a new compact with the unions.

For the Social Democrat Government rightly insisted that the way to safeguard the welfare state and to return to full employment was for employees not to receive full compansation for increased prices arising from devaluation. In other words, welfare and employment should be given priority over wage increases. But the Social Democrats also stressed that sacrifices should be distributed as fairly as possible. The increases in taxes on the wealthy and the introduction of employee investment funds, were also necessary for trade union acceptance of the wage restraint, in turn wage restraint led to the higher profitability needed to generate increased investment, output and employment. In short, the Swedish solidarity strategy was essential for economic recovery.

The *West German* solidarity system was less structured than either the Austrian or the Swedish but was nevertheless a highly important factor in Social Democrat success. A key feature of the system was the significance attached by both the SPD and the trade unions to industrial democracy. The 'co-determination' laws of 1951 and 1952 had established a structure of one-third employee representation on the board of all German companies, except in coal and steel in which there was equality of representation. As we have seen in 1973, the Brandt Government strengthened workers' rights at shop-floor level by the Works Constitution Law. Then, in 1976, a compromise deal on board-level representatives greatly increased influence.

Ironically, it was the employers' legal challenge to the 1976 legislation which led to the withdrawal in 1977 of the German Trade Union Federation (DGB) from 'concerted action', the series of consultative conferences between government, unions and employers set up by the SPD Minister of Economics, Karl Schiller, in 1967. 'Concerted action' was never a formal incomes policy arrangement but it did ensure that collective bargaining took place within a broadly agreed view of the direction of the economy and the relationships between full employment, output and inflation. Even before 1977, however, the formality of concerted action had been supplemented, if not replaced, by informal but regular meetings between the Chancellor, Helmut Schmidt, and the trade unions and employers.[17] In addition, Schmidt always maintained close personal contact with trade union leaders.

Incomes policy or no incomes policy, German trade unions continued to agree to moderate wage settlements not merely because they fully accepted the relationship between wage and price increases but also because they recognised that such a strategy was one of the pre-conditions for the success of Schmidt's *Modell Deutschland* and the defence of the welfare services, labour market policies, and co-determination at work which both the SPD and the unions supported so fervently. In their view, social gains could only be preserved by social discipline.

The contrast with what happened to the *British Labour* Government's efforts to forge an effective and enduring compact with the unions is obvious. The social contract of 1974–9 was an ambitious attempt to link together social welfare, tax policy, output, employment and incomes in a coherent whole. If its initial phase (until July 1975) took too little account of wage increases, it had considerable success over the next three years in reducing inflation. And there were significant gains for large families and pensioners, as with extensions of rights for employees and trade unions at the workplace.

However, British Labour's solidarity model was undermined by the 'winter of discontent' of 1978–9. In part, this was the fault of the Government which asked too much at the wrong time. But the trade unions' acceptance of the 'social contract' idea was, in any case, always conditional. To many British trade unionists a moderate wages policy was not an integral part of a comprehensive and long-term system of 'trade-offs' but a short-term sacrifice in an immediate economic crisis. Once the crisis was over, they were prepared and eager to return to more traditional types of collective bargaining in which linkages were less overt.

Both the *French* and *Spanish* Socialist governments also tried to create solidarity systems. The French government set up a Ministry of 'National Solidarity' in 1983, and consulted regularly with the trade unions, while the Spanish Government succeeded in October 1984 in setting up an Economic and Social Agreement which was signed by government, trade unions and employers and linked wage increases, social benefits and employment-creation in one package.

But these two governments faced a similar problem in establishing a lasting system. In both France and Spain the trade union movements were relatively weak and divided. In France only about 25 per cent of the labour force was organised, while in Spain the equivalent figure was nearer 18 per cent. In both countries there was a strong Communist trade union – in France it was the most powerful, while in Spain it was about equal in size to the Socialist trade union. The difficulties arising from Communist trade union strength was illustrated in France when, after the Communist Ministers resigned in July 1984, the Confédération Générale du Travail (CGT) came out in opposition to the Socialist Government; in Spain the Communist union, the Comisiones Obreras (CCOO), refused to sign the AES in October 1984 and in 1985 put pressure on the Socialist union to strike against the Socialists' pensions legislation and oppose the government's economic policies.

CONCLUSION

Despite the intellectual attack on public spending and the difficulties of the recession, European Socialists maintained their belief in and their support for welfare. German and Swedish Social Democrat governments effectively preserved their social spending programmes, while the Austrian Socialists were actually able to introduce improvements. Even when, as in the case of British Labour and the Mitterrand administration in France, Socialist governments were forced on the defensive, they still managed to protect the weakest social groups, such as pensioners and poor families, from the worst effects of the recession.

Solidarity strategies which linked together economic and social policies and were based on agreement with trade unions were a prominent feature of the recession period, particularly in Austria, Sweden and West Germany, though they were also present in Britain, France and Spain. Significantly, welfare was seen not only as a way of protecting the less well off and providing essential services, such as health and education, but also, as in Schmidt's West Germany, of preserving a common purpose in difficult times. In the revised Swedish Social Democrat model, social spending was viewed not as an obstacle to economic change but as an effective way of promoting it. In the hard times, the welfare state was more than ever relevant.

11 Foreign Policies: Hanging Together

'No Western country – not even the largest – can assure its prosperity by its own efforts along.'[1] To a great extent, this limitation on autonomy in the economic sphere (emphasised by Robert Putnam and Nicholas Bayne in describing the attempts of the major Western powers to coordinate their economic policies during the recession) also applied in the international political, strategic and defence fields.

Clearly the two superpowers still retained considerable freedom of action. But in the 1970s and 1980s both the United States and the Soviet Union ran up against the limits to their power – in Vietnam and Afghanistan, to quote the two most obvious examples. For medium-sized countries (like West Germany, France and Britain), the scope for independent activity was severely restrained by geo-strategic, political, demographic and economic realities. Increasingly, these countries, as well as smaller ones, sought to exert influence through regional and international groupings, such as the EEC, NATO, OECD, GATT and the UN.

The rationale for such collaboration was not only to supply an alternative to independent action, but also to provide greater security in an uncertain world. In the 1970s and 80s, there was great concern, particularly expressed by Socialists, about the dangers of the nuclear arms race. In addition, there was the necessity for more international cooperation, again most passionately advocated by Socialists, to revive the Western economies and to fight world poverty and starvation.

Yet, if the ability to act independently was limited and the case for acting together compelling, the obstacles to cooperation remained formidable. Varying ideological and policy positions and the pressures of domestic politics as well as different perceptions of national interest all made effective coordination hard to achieve.

It is against this background of limited power, conflicting national views and interests, and growing uncertainty that we must judge the foreign policies of Socialist governments in the

1970s and 1980s. Denis Healey has written that 'our main task as Socialists is to establish some collective democratic control over the international anarchy on the basis of greater economic and political equality between the richer and poorer countries.'[2] This is a highly desirable foreign policy objective but it has to be remembered that the ability to influence external affairs of socialist administrations (and indeed governments of any other complexions) in Austria, Sweden, Spain, Britain, France and even in West Germany, remained heavily circumscribed throughout the recession years.

SCHMIDT'S WEST GERMANY: RELUCTANT EUROPEAN GREAT POWER

As has already been noted (see Chapter 3), Helmut Schmidt's period as Chancellor coincided with the emergence in the mid-1970s of the Federal Republic as a European great power. West Germany's increased economic strength, combined with her strategic importance as the possessor of the largest conventional forces in Western Europe and her geographic position between East and West gave the SPD-led coalition the opportunity of and responsibility for pursuing a more active foreign policy.

Yet it was the foreign policy of a reluctant European great power, not of a country which was attempting to behave like a superpower. 'I am speaking on behalf of a country that cannot and will not act as a big power,' declared Schmidt in a speech to the UN General Assembly in May, 1978. Wary of independent initiatives, Schmidt worked through alliances and international organisations, through the EEC, NATO, the OECD, and the new Western economic summits which he had helped set up, as well as the established relationships with France, the United States and the Eastern bloc countries. But, as Schmidt told the SPD foreign policy conference in January 1985, in the new situation created by increased German power, 'We simply cannot avoid affirming our co-responsibility for the economic welfare of other countries.'

Schmidt's inheritance from his predecessors was twofold: first, the secure base in the Western alliance created by Konrad Adenauer; secondly, the opened channels of *Ostpolitik* and greater diplomatic freedom towards the East created under the

Chancellorship of Willy Brandt. Schmidt explained West Germany's dual position as follows:

> We are a member of the Western alliance, we want to see the alliance maintain its strength. . . to think of the alliance without Germany is to think of fairly little. . .on the other hand, one of the necessities of the alliance as well as for us Germans is to get along with the Eastern powers. . .there is nothing to be gained for the Germans in a cold war, divided as our nation is, divided as our capital of Berlin is.[3]

Both elements – membership of the Alliance and *Ostpolitik* – contributed to West German and European security.

Schmidt was a strong supporter of detente in Europe. He set up regular meetings with the Soviet leader Leonid Brezhnev, came to an agreement in August 1975 with the Polish government whereby 120 000 Poles of German origin were allowed to travel to the West, and established personal contacts with Eduard Gierek and Janos Kadar, the Polish and Hungarian leaders. In 1980, a German foreign policy expert reminded a congressional committee in Washington of the benefits of detente, of 'those eight million West Germans that can now annually go to East Germany, those 1.5 million East Germans annually visiting the West, or the 60 000 German emigrants we extract every year out of East Europe'.[4]

However, the Chancellor also became concerned about the nuclear balance in Europe. The Strategic Arms Limitation Accord of 1971 (SALT I) had codified the nuclear balance between the superpowers in the intercontinental range, but it excluded intermediate missiles in Europe where the Soviet Union had a decisive advantage. In Schmidt's view, the introduction of the Soviet SS20 missiles, far superior to previous Soviet weapons, brought into question the credibility of the Western deterrent system in Europe. Would the United States be ready to reply with an intercontinental missile to a Soviet attack with an intermediate weapon on Hamburg, if that meant the risk of losing Chicago? Schmidt's misgivings were compounded by his misunderstandings over a number of issues with the American President, Jimmy Carter, whom Schmidt felt 'was just not big enough for the game'.[5]

In October 1977, Schmidt raised his doubts publicly in a speech at the International Institute for Strategic Studies in

London in which he urged that NATO should be ready to increase its nuclear capability in Europe. It was this speech and subsequent German pressure which led to Carter's agreement to deployment of Cruise and Pershing missiles at the 'Big Four' talks at Guadeloupe in January 1979 and the controversial NATO 'twin-track' decision in December by which it was agreed to deploy 572 intermediate missiles in Western Europe, while at the same time calling on Moscow to negotiate mutual reductions or even a complete scrapping of these weapons.

But Schmidt's support for the deployment of Cruise and Pershing missiles in Western Europe did not mean that he changed his mind on detente. On the contrary, it was Schmidt who, after the invasion of Afghanistan in January 1980, argued that Russia must be given time to change its mind, who visited East Germany in December 1981 despite Poland's internal crisis (to his embarrassment he was still in East Germany when martial law was imposed in Poland) and who led the successful opposition in 1981–82 to Reagan's attempts to block the Soviet-West European natural gas pipeline deal. In his farewell to the diplomatic corps on 30 September 1982 he ended with these words: 'Peace is not a natural state but one that must be ever re-established. . .to strengthen confidence in the consistency of our policy for peace – that was the contribution I wished to make.'[6]

Perhaps the major contribution of West Germany under Schmidt was in the field of world economic affairs. The events of 1974–5 had underlined the dependence of West Germany on the health of the world economy (see Chapters 2 and 5). Schmidt therefore lent his full weight to the idea of regular summits of the seven major OECD countries to provide a new Western economic leadership and to coordinate national economic policies. If his overriding concern was to prevent a slide into pro-tectionism (so inimical to West Germany's interests as one of the major trade nations), in 1977–8 he also gave his backing to refla-tion. As we have seen at the 1977 London summit, the West Germans committed themselves to a 5 per cent growth target, which as a result of the 1978 Bonn summit agreement the Federal Government introduced a DM 12.5 billion pump-priming pro-gramme. This reflation was not only in the interests of Germany's partners like Britain and Italy, but was also in the interests of Germany as well. Schmidt was advised shortly before the Bonn summit that 'if the Federal Republic takes part in such a concerted action, it does so, not out of altruism, but out of solid national interest'.[7]

The creation of the European Monetary System (EMS) in March 1979 was, as was pointed out in Chapter 3, an attempt by Schmidt and Giscard to shield the European currencies from dollar-induced currency shocks and to create regional monetary stability in an unstable world of floating exchange rates and erratic dollar movements. Of course, there was a strong German interest in a stable deutschmark but Schmidt genuinely believed that currency instability had become a major obstacle to world growth. If the United States was not prepared to provide the necessary leadership, West Germany, acting with her partners, had an obligation to take the initiative.

There are legitimate doubts about some of Schmidt's decisions – for example in resisting reflation for too long, in initiating the idea of Western deployment of new theatre nuclear weapons in Europe, in thinking that detente in Central Europe could be divorced from what was happening elsewhere. But in the reluctant assumption of the responsibilities of a European great power, West Germany, under the Chancellorship of Helmut Schmidt, behaved like a good neighbour. As he himself said in his final political testament. 'I warn against thinking that one can solve one's problems by a policy pursued at the cost of others.'[8]

BRITISH LABOUR GOVERNMENTS 1974–9: LEARNING TO BUILD BRIDGES

While the SPD-led coalition in West Germany was forced by its strengthened position to play a greater role in the world, the British Labour Governments (1974–9) found that domestic economic difficulties not only impaired their attempts to exercise British influence but also obliged them to concentrate to a considerable extent on international economic issues.

The Labour party fought the two general elections of 1974 on six main foreign policy planks: strengthening international institutions, supporting liberation movements, increasing aid to developing countries, working for independence and majority rule in Rhodesia, reducing defence spending and negotiating the terms of entry to the EEC, to be followed by a referendum on the result.

The EEC renegotiation policy was devised partly for internal party and partly electoral reasons. But James Callaghan, then Foreign Secretary, also believed that a better financial deal for the United Kingdom and improved access for Commonwealth dairy products could be negotiated without confrontation, and in fact he achieved some modifications. Although the Labour party at a special conference in 1975 came out against the renegotiated settlement and in favour of withdrawal, the Labour Government argued that the deal was the best possible in the circumstances and recommended it to the British people. The June 1975 referendum resulted in a large majority for remaining within the Community.

Even so, the Government had difficulty in finding its feet within the EEC. This was in part because Britain continued to make a wholly disproportionate budgetary contribution to a European Community dominated by the Common Agricultural Policy. In 1979, Britain – which was seventh out of nine in per capita income – was the largest contributor to the Community budget. In part, it was also because the British were used to playing a more independent foreign policy role. For example, in 1975 Harold Wilson tried and failed to get a separate British seat at the Paris North–South Conference between energy producers and consumers. The Labour Government's refusal to join the EMS in 1979 was founded on stronger grounds. Callaghan feared that such a system might make German exports even more competitive and tie Britain to an unrealistic exchange rate. He also did not wish to be seen to 'gang up' on the United States. But the problem for the Labour Government was that, in preserving an independent line over the EMS, it ran the risk of leaving the leadership of the EEC in the hands of the French and Germans.

Callaghan saw the British role as one of building bridges – between her main ally, the United States, and the Europeans, between Europe and the developing world, between East and West. 'The EEC gives us a firm base from which to work. The Commonwealth offers a unique bridge across the divisions of mankind. . .the UN offers an instrument for global co-operation provided we have the political will to use it.'[9] In the 1970s Labour's aims were, however, difficult to achieve. Despite Henry

Kissinger's shuttle diplomacy and British support for the American initiative, the Rhodesian problem was not settled during Labour's term of office. Although aid was protected from the rounds of cuts, the Government failed to increase aid as a share of GDP. The emphasis on international human rights, though welcome, was more rhetoric than achievement. And, although Labour gave consistent support to detente and to the Strategic Arms Limitations talks between the United States and the Soviet Union, her position was always less influential than that of the West Germans.

The British, however, played a significant part in the economic summits, particularly at London in 1977 and Bonn in 1978. In 1976 the Labour Government had had to endure long and bruising negotiations with the IMF over budget cuts. It was, therefore, essential both politically and economically that the London summit came out strongly in favour of economic expansion. The Labour Government's strategy was for the strong economies with low inflation and large balance of payments surpluses to expand in order to provide a 'locomotive' for world recovery. With the backing of the new American administration, Callaghan and Healey urged the Germans and the Japanese to reflate to prevent weaker countries turning to protection and 'beggar-my-neighbour' policies. Schmidt restated his concern about inflation and insisted on inserting the phrase that 'inflation does not reduce unemployment. . .on the contrary, it is one of its major causes' in the final communique. However at London both the Germans and the Japanese for the first time committed themselves to a growth target. Although their targets were not met, the commitments made by Schmidt and the Japanese Prime Minister were critical to the successful outcome of the Bonn summit the following year.

Callaghan played a crucial mediating role in putting together the Bonn package.[10] In the early part of 1978, US–German relations had deteriorated over a number of issues, including the need for German expansion, the decline of the dollar, US dependence on foreign oil, and Carter's cancellation of the neutron bomb. In March 1978, Callaghan visited Bonn and Washington to suggest the outlines of a deal at the July summit. The Germans would accelerate growth, the Americans would agree to conserve energy and share more broadly the burdens of managing the international monetary system, the French and British would liberalise trade, and all would increase aid to the Third World. One authoritative comment on Callaghan's initiative was that it 'was an important step forward and contained virtually all the elements of the eventual Bonn settlement'.[11] Bonn was a notable success, albeit an isolated one, for British diplomacy and for the 'bridge building' role on which Callaghan had laid such stress.

MITTERRAND SEARCHES FOR A CONSTRUCTIVE ROLE

Like the British Labour Government, the French Socialist administration found it difficult to exert its country's influence. As we have seen, the presidency of Francois Mitterrand was pre-occupied with domestic economic problems; he also had to operate in a hostile and unstable international environment.

The Socialist President, like De Gaulle before him, made it quite clear that he believed France had an important role to play on the world stage. At his inaugural, Mitterrand stressed that a great nation should only entertain what he called 'noble projects', and that France should enlighten 'humanity's progress'. The new Foreign Minister, Claude Cheysson, put French foreign policy aims in a more prosaic way. The nation, he said, had to accept that

> there could not be a foreign policy for a country such as France but rather a translation of internal policy into external terms. . . .the internal priority should be employment, and this concern translated into external terms would mean inproving relations with trading partners. It would mean making full use of the large EC market, developing the huge political markets in the third world with arrangements such as the Lomé Convention, and seeking a more co-operative attitude from the US over interest rates policy.

In matters of defence and security, Mitterrand took a firm stance. His election manifesto, the '110 propositions', had said little about defence, apart from support for the so-called 'zero' option of simultaneous withdrawal of the Soviet SS-20 missiles and cancellation of Pershing and Cruise missiles. However, in October 1981, the new government committed itself to maintaining a French nuclear strike force, and confirmed the construction of a seventh nuclear submarine. Almost immediately after his election, Mitterrand had also lent his support to deployment of Cruise and Pershing: 'I believe that peace is linked to the balance of forces in the world. The installation of SS-20s and the Backfires has disturbed this balance in Europe. I cannot accept this and I believe that Europe must rearm in order to reestablish equilibrium.'[12] In January 1983 in a speech to the Bundestag, Mitterrand urged the Germans to support the presence of Pershings on their soil.

There were three reasons for Mitterrand's defence strategy. First, De Gaulle's decision to withdraw French forces from NATO's military command and to remove foreign bases and troops from French soil had changed Socialist attitudes to the idea of a French nuclear force. For example, Ceres, the left-wing Socialist faction, argued for withdrawal from the Atlantic Alliance *and* the development of a powerful French nuclear deterrent. Secondly, the French Socialists had come to power at a time when detente had virtually collapsed. The Russians were deploying SS-20s, Afghanistan had been invaded, NATO had taken its twin-track decision, and the superpowers were committed to a major escalation of the nuclear arms race. Mitterrand believed that only the certainty of deployment of Cruise and Pershing would bring the Russians to the negotiating table. Thirdly, the French President may also have felt that support for President Reagan's nuclear policy would help neutralise American opposition to the expansionary economic policy of the French Government (particularly one with Communist participation) and make the United States more receptive to French concern about the level of US interest rates and the strength of the dollar. As he observed, 'one cannot hope for political and military cohesion in the Atlantic Alliance and be content with an everyman-for-himself attitude in economics'.[13]

However, French hopes for an American change of line in international economic policy were disappointed. At the 1981 Ottawa summit, the communique praised 'low and stable monetary growth', stressed the need 'urgently to reduce public borrowing' and called for lowered expectations. At the 1982 Versailles summit, which Mitterrand hosted, macroeconomics was discussed surprisingly little. Mitterrand, who knew that within days he would be forced to announce a more restrictive domestic stance, had to be content with an unsatisfactory compromise over exchange rate policy, by which it was agreed to study the effectiveness of past central bank interventions in the currency markets. The 1983 Williamsburg summit, with its support for conservative economic policies, merely underlined France's isolation. Despite all his efforts, Mitterrand had failed to find any major allies for his ideas of coordinated economic expansion and a new Bretton Woods conference to reconstruct the world's monetary system.[14]

Although the French Socialist Government took a tough position on defence, over the Russian invasion of Afghanistan, and over the Polish crisis, it strongly opposed the United States' attempt to block East-West trade and the projected gas pipeline from the Soviet Union to Western Europe. In Central America, Mitterrand also made clear French condemnation of US strategy, declaring that the guerrilla movements there were genuine popular revolts. Europe should assist Central America in combatting poverty, disease and repression. In August 1981 France signed a joint declaration with Mexico recognising the El Salvadorean guerrillas as a 'legitimate representative force' and calling for a political solution to that country's problems. This initiative was followed up by the sale of arms to Nicaragua. In general, the French Government stressed the need for a new approach to third world countries, including increasing both aid and trade and argued that North–South problems should be given as much attention as East–West ones.

But, as might be expected, the French were perhaps most influential within the EEC. At the heart of Mitterrand's EEC strategy, like that of his predecessors, was the Franco-German alliance. Mitterrand, as Giscard with Schmidt, developed a personal relationship with the German Chancellor – the Christian Democrat, Helmut Kohl. To cement the friendship a Franco-German defence commission was established to consider a number of issues, including using the French rapid deployment forces on German soil. With Britain, Mitterrand's relations were correct, if cool. However, the fact that, in 1984, the EEC was prepared to go some way to meet the British case for easing the burden of her financial contribution owed much to Mittrand's determination to produce a lasting solution to the problem of British membership.

If it was the Germans who had the most to lose financially by the settlement of the British budget dispute, the French, and particularly the Socialists, had something to lose by Spanish entry to the Community. Once again it was Mitterrand who broke the deadlock by agreeing, after some delays, to put the cause of Spanish democracy before French wine producers and tomato growers. And the subsequent efforts, following enlargement, to move the EEC forward politically were spearheaded by the French President and his support for majority voting. Within the EEC, if not outside, Mitterrand's France successfully played a constructive role.

SPANISH SOCIALIST FOREIGN POLICY: COMING IN FROM THE COLD

The Spanish Socialist party inherited a foreign policy from the UCD governments which, on the whole, they were prepared to accept – though quick to stress that a Socialist Government would provide a different emphasis on various aspects of that policy. One clear difference of approach lay over the question of NATO, which Spain had joined in unseemly haste, so the Socialists argued, in the previous spring. PSOE announced that a referendum would be held on the question of NATO at an appropriate time.

Perhaps the overriding consideration in the foreign policy of the new Spanish democracy was the need to end her diplomatic isolation and protect her fragile political institutions. By the 1980s the case for Spanish entry to the EEC, still unresolved when the Socialists came to power, was put in primarily political terms. Indeed, the economic arguments were finely balanced.[15] It was generally recognised that entry could create considerable difficulties for Spanish industry, while, although there were obvious opportunities for Mediterranean fruit and vegetable growers within the EEC, Spain was a major net agricultural importer. But all Spanish political parties, including the Socialists, believed that membership of the EEC would 'eliminate the stigma of Spain's exclusion from the European decision-making process caused by the unacceptability of the Franco regime', serve as a 'badge of modernity', and act as 'a political insurance for democracy'.[16]

Felipe Gonzalez and his Foreign Minister, Fernando Moran, put all the prestige and authority of the Government behind the effort to join the EEC. After two and a half years of negotiation and delay, the Spanish finally succeeded in overcoming French and Italian misgivings. Spain, together with Portugal, joined the EEC on 1 January 1986. The key to Spanish entry lay in Paris. It was Moran, an experienced diplomat, who played a decisive role in improving relations with the French government. Moran also came to an agreement with Britain in November 1984 over the way to handle the Gibraltar question. However, despite Moran's contribution, he was replaced in July 1985.

Gonzalez moved Moran because the Foreign Minister remained unenthusiastic about Spanish membership of NATO. Despite PSOE's opposition to joining NATO, Gonzalez announced in October 1984 that the Government would argue in favour of the case for staying in at the referendum. There were probably two main reasons for the change of mind. The first was external. There is some evidence that West German and Italian leaders made it clear that they would not support Spanish entry to the EEC, if, at the same time, Spain was about to leave NATO.[17] Gonzalez had to declare where he stood on NATO in advance of a successful conclusion of the EEC negotiations. The second reason was internal. The statement by Narcis Serra, the Defence Minister, in January 1985 that withdrawal would be 'very difficult' was in part a reference to the impact on the army of leaving NATO. While membership of NATO was no guarantee against a military coup, it did at least help focus the attention of the armed forces on Spain's borders rather than on Madrid.

However, in their successful referendum campaign, the government's most effective, if somewhat questionable, public argument was that withdrawal would hit exports and investments which, as they pointed out, were to a considerable extent dependent on trade relations with NATO members. At the same time, Gonzalez, acknowledging the strength of anti-American feeling, stressed the European side of NATO as an alternative to bilateral defence ties with the United States. Significantly, the statement of the government's case on the ballot paper emphasised that Spanish participation in the Atlantic Alliance would not include its incorporation in the integrated military structure, that the ban on installing, storing or introducing nuclear arms would be maintained, and that a progressive reduction of the United States military presence in Spain would be undertaken.

Relations with Washington were finely balanced. As well as deciding to stay in NATO, the Government bought American fighter bombers, and endorsed the NATO twin-track decision on European missiles. However, Gonzalez also made no secret of the fact that he opposed American foreign policy in Central America. He consistently argued that the Americans were wrong to see the problems there simply in terms of East–West struggle, and pointed out that it was much more a battle against poverty and social inequality than a fight between Marxism and Western democracies. With this as his central thesis he supported the Contadora group of nations (Mexico, Columbia, Venezuela, Panama) in their attempts to reach some sort of compromise between the opposing forces.

There is no doubt that the Spanish Socialists wished to play a greater role in South and Central America. This was partly because they felt that Spain had a special affinity with Latin America. They believed that the country's peaceful transition from dictatorship to democracy could serve as a model for the area. At the same time, Gonzalez was aware that should Spain be called upon to act as an honest broker it would enhance Spanish prestige, and thereby add status to the standing of his Government.

SWEDEN AND AUSTRIA: ACTIVE NEUTRALITY

During the recession years, Sweden and Austria maintained their neutral stance. But, under Socialist Governments, neutrality was interpreted in an active rather than passive way.

Swedish neutrality was of long standing and had the support of all political parties. As a matter of free choice, Sweden had decided not to participate in alliances and had stayed out of both world wars. Austrian neutrality, though initiated by the Socialists, was imposed by the 1955 State Treaty signed by the four occupying powers.

The Austrian State Treaty limited Austrian armed forces. In contrast, the defence of Swedish neutrality involved building a strong and costly defence system – a policy which was firmly supported by the Social Democrats. In the recession, defence programmes were maintained, and Swedish politicians, including Social Democrats, continued to assert the need for a strong defence. In September 1984, Prime Minister Olof Palme protested strongly against Soviet violations of Swedish territory. He reminded the Soviet Union that good relations required 'full respect for territorial integrity'. He also told pacifists in his own party that neutrality had to be defended.

If Austria and Sweden were neutrals, they remained closely linked to the West. Both countries had joined the Council of Europe. Both countries were members of EFTA and had signed free trade agreements with the European Community. In the recession, both countries used the OECD as a forum to urge greater economic coordination among industrial countries, and both joined the International Energy Agency set up under OECD auspices to evolve a common response to the first oil shock. Kreisky put the position succinctly: 'Neutrality not neutralism. We are part of the Western world.'

However, the Swedish Social Democrats as well as the Austrian Socialists remained active propagators of detente and disarmament. In 1984 Sweden hosted the Stockholm Conference on confidence and security building measures and disarmament in Europe, while Austria which, under the inspiration of Kreisky, had pioneered the policy of normalising relations with Eastern bloc neighbours, spoke out firmly against the deterioration in East/West relations and the renewed arms race. Under Kreisky, Vienna became not only a major new centre for UN organisations but also a meeting place for world leaders.

Kreisky, in particular, developed Austrian neutrality as a mediating force. Henry Kissinger commented that Kreisky 'packaged his country's formal neutrality into a position of influence beyond its strength, often by interpreting the motives of competing countries to each other'.[18] After the Yom Kippur war, Kreisky, at the invitation of the Socialist International, led a mission to the Arab world. He built up contacts with the Palestinians and formulated peace plans for the Middle East.

Both Austria and Sweden also played a prominent part in the North–South dialogue. The Swedish record of assistance to developing countries was one which few other countries could match. Despite budget difficulties, the Social Democrat Government elected in 1982 maintained international aid at 1 per cent of gross national income. It also made special efforts to help the poorest countries, particularly those burdened with debt. Sweden and Austria supported the demands of developing countries for changes in the international economic order. Palme, like Kreisky, believed that Socialist Governments should promote greater international social and economic justice.

CONCLUSION

During the recession, Socialist Governments laid greater stress than before on international cooperation. This was in part because of the limitations on their ability to act independently. Equally important, however, was their concern about threats to security and the dangers arising from the nuclear arms race, as well as the need to act together to revive the world economic system.

Socialist administrations in former great powers, such as Britain and France, argued for more effective international collaboration. The Labour Government stayed in the European Community, made an important contribution to the successful outcome of the 1978 Bonn economic summit and saw the British role as one of 'bridge-building'. The Mitterrand Government, despite the Gaullist inheritance and the retention of a French nuclear force, tried desperately to persuade more conservative governments of the benefits of coordinated economic expansion and played a constructive role within the European economic community. The main foreign policy objective (an objective which was triumphantly achieved) of the Spanish Social Government was to end their country's isolation by joining the European community.

Under Helmut Schmidt, the new European great power, West Germany, acted almost exclusively through international institutions and alliances. If it was right for Germany to assume new responsibilities, it was significant that she did so in cooperation with her neighbours, both in the West and in the East.

Although many of the initiatives of Socialist Governments were firmly based on national interest and there remained formidable obstacles to effective coordination, there was undoubtedly a greater awareness than ever before among Socialists that in the 1970s and 1980s it was better to hang together than to hang separately.

12   Democratic Socialism: For the Good Times and the Bad Times

It is now possible to answer more clearly the question posed in the introduction – how far is democratic socialism a 'fair weather' philosophy which is doomed to decline and failure when hard times come?

In the first chapter, the pattern of socialism in the highly favourable conditions of the 1950s and 1960s was characterised as follows: Keynesian economic policies and an element of economic and industrial intervention to maintain activity and employment, a high level of social spending to ensure that the less well off groups shared the fruits of growth, educational reform to provide better opportunities for working-class children, partnership with the unions (particularly over incomes), and a collaborative and cooperative approach to relations with other countries. This interventionist and egalitarian approach was not only successful in sustaining full employment and growth and in creating a fairer social system but was also politically and intellectually dominant until the recession.

NOT SO DIFFERENT

In the recession years, the ideas and policies of Socialists were challenged by the right. As inflation persisted and unemployment soared, it became fashionable to argue that Keynesian economic policies and social spending programmes were both harmful and irrelevant in the new conditions. Yet, despite these criticisms, the policies pursued by Socialist governments during the recession were recognisably based on or derived from the strategies of the 1950s and 1960s.

Take Keynesian policies: although Helmut Schmidt's SPD-led coalition relied on a mix of economic measures, it introduced a number of fiscal packages which were very much in the Keynesian tradition, while Chancellor Kreisky of Austria never made any secret of his belief in the need for budget deficits during recession. In the harsher economic and political environment after 1979, it became more difficult as both the French and Spanish Socialists in their different ways found out, to pursue expansionist policies. Indeed, the Swedish 'third way' of 1982, based on a big devaluation, was a conscious attempt to replace the boost of an increase in internal demand (ruled out because of larger budget and balance of payment deficits) by the stimulus provided by a change in the exchange rate. Even so, the examples of the Austrian Socialist Government and, to a considerable extent, of the French Socialists in the later 'austerity' period demonstrated that there was still a place, in spite of the hostile international environment, for policies which gave priority to protecting employment.

During the recession, Socialists also continued to support the welfare idea, despite the attacks of Conservatives and the difficulties of financing social programmes. German and Swedish Social Democrat governments effectively preserved social spending, while the Austrian Socialists were able to introduce improvements. Even when, as with British Labour and the Mitterrand administration in France, Socialist governments were forced on the defensive, they still managed to protect the weakest social groups, such as pensioners and poor families.

'Solidarity' strategies which linked together economic and social policies and were based on agreement with trade unions were increasingly prominent, particularly in Austria, Sweden and West Germany, though they were also a feature in Britain, France and Spain. Significantly, welfare spending was seen not only as a way of protecting the less well off and providing the essential services, such as health and education, but, as in the case of Schmidt's West Germany, of preserving a common purpose and unity in difficult conditions. In their revised model, Swedish Social Democrats also argued that mobility and change were much easier to achieve against a backing of security of employment and welfare than in a high unemployment, low welfare economy. In the bad times, Socialists demonstrated that the welfare state was more than ever relevant.

In contrast to the 1930s when isolationism and nationalism had been the common reactions, Socialists in the 1970s and

1980s laid even greater emphasis than before on international cooperation. This was in part because of the limitations on their ability to act independently. But it was also because of their concern about the nuclear arms race and the threats to security, as well as the need to act together to revive the world economic system.

The new 'European Great Power', West Germany, worked almost exclusively through international institutions and alliances while, under Socialist governments, Spain joined the European Community, Britain continued a member, and France, despite the influence of Gaullist ideas, played a constructive role. Another feature was the attempt to secure greater economic coordination. At the summit meetings of the major industrial countries, West German Social Democrat, British Labour and French Socialist governments all strongly backed the idea of concerted economic expansion.

If there was one political idea which best characterised the approach of Socialists in the recession, it was that of solidarity. Significantly, Socialists were not merely concerned with party or class solidarity but with the need to develop the maximum possible common purpose throughout society. The case for welfare was no longer argued solely on egalitarian grounds but increasingly because it would help maintain social cohesion. Arguably, the Socialism of the 1950s and 1960s had been about social justice and sharing out the fruits of growths. In the 1970s and 1980s, Socialism was more about solidarity and common purpose and obligation.

ACHIEVEMENTS AND LIMITATIONS

The achievements of Socialist governments during the recession were, in many ways, impressive. For example, the record of Socialist governments on unemployment was superior to that of most other types of administration. Socialist Austria and Social Democratic Sweden consistently maintained the lowest levels of unemployment in the OECD area.[1] Even when as, in the case of France and Britain, Socialist administrations were blown off course, they still managed to prevent unemployment increasing as fast as in a number of other countries. In 1979 when British Labour left office the unemployment level was around average for the major OECD countries[2], while President Mitterrand's

France had a better unemployment performance than either Mrs Thatcher's Britain or Chancellor Kohl's West Germany.[3] In Spain the Socialists were unable to prevent unemployment rising but they had inherited an economy which was badly out of balance.

What was especially significant was that, in most cases, these administrations managed to combine better than average records on both unemployment and inflation. Austria, throughout the period, and West Germany, under Helmut Schmidt, performed especially well. France, under Mitterrand, managed to bring down the rate of inflation from 13.5 per cent in 1981 to under 5 per cent by the end of 1985 without paying the cost in unemployment suffered in Britain under Mrs Thatcher.

Socialist administrations also gave a much higher priority to welfare. The achievement in Austria, West Germany and Sweden was particularly noteworthy, while even in France and Britain the weakest groups were given special protection. More generally, these governments emphasised social consensus and the need for all groups to work together at a time when many Conservatives were pursuing much more divisive policies.

The most effective Socialist governments were those which, as in West Germany, Austria and Sweden, had the most fully developed 'solidarity' systems. It was these governments which most successfully combined low levels of unemployment and inflation with a high level of social spending and welfare. If the benefits were clear, it was equally obvious that when such agreements were less developed, as in France and Spain, or broke down, as in Britain, it was far more difficult to achieve such multiple objectives. Even so, incomes policies were successful in bringing down inflation from 1975 to 1978 in Britain and from 1983 onwards in France.

In chapter 2, it was shown how, as a consequence of the growing interdependence of modern industrial economies, the ability of governments to influence their own output has been reduced and their vulnerability to outside events has increased. Socialist administrations in the three major West European economies – West Germany, France and Britain – fully understood the compelling case for greater national coordination. At the 1978 Bonn summit, led by Helmut Schmidt and James Callaghan and with the support of a sympathetic American President, the seven largest industrial countries successfully put together a reflationary package which had a significant impact on world output. The failure of President Mitterrand to persuade more conservative leaders of the need to take similar action was one of the reasons why the recession of the 1980s was deeper and more prolonged than that of the 1970s. It was clear that a more coordinated international approach had become essential if individual economies were to achieve a higher growth rate and reduce unemployment faster.

CONCLUSION: THE APPEAL OF SOLIDARITY

By the mid-1980s European Democratic Socialism had demonstrated that it was not merely a philosophy for the prosperous times but was equally relevant when the economic climate changed.

The argument that there was no longer the class base or moral imperative for the survival of socialism was confounded by the political, economic and social achievements of European Socialist parties during the 1970s and 1980s. The success of the German Social Democrats and the Austrian Socialists, and, to a lesser extent, of the British Labour party in the 1970s, the comeback of the Swedish Social Democrats, the continuing hold on office of the Austrian Socialists, and the advent to power of the Socialists in France and Spain in the 1980s is, at the very least, an indication that there were not inexorable long-term forces which made decline inevitable.

Of course, there were modifications in the social composition of many European countries, some but by no means all of which worked against Socialist parties.[4] One common feature was the tendency as a result of economic and social change for the proportion of the manual workers in the total electorate to decrease. Yet, despite this development, Socialists continued to be the majority party in Austria and Sweden, gained power for the first time in France and Spain, and were the main parties of opposition in West Germany and Britain. Socialist leaders like Palme, Kreisky, Schmidt, Gonzalez and Mitterrand were able to appeal beyond the ranks of their traditional support on the basis of their parties' values, policies and overall credibility and competence.

At a time when persistent recession put industrial societies under considerable strain, a political approach which, in contrast to the unbalanced and divisive individualism of the right, stressed the need for cooperation and social harmony was bound to have appeal. Similarly, interventionist economic policies which sought to combine low unemployment, low inflation and high output, social policies which gave priority to welfare, community programmes and consensus building, and foreign policies which worked for industrial cooperation and peace were clearly relevant. No wonder that European Democratic Socialism remained such a powerful political force.

References

Introduction

1. Peter Jenkins, *The Sunday Times*, 15 December 1985.

1 Socialism before the Recession

1. Francis Castles, *The Social Democratic Image of Society* (London: Routledge & Kegan Paul, 1978) pp. 16–17.
2. H. Tingsten, *The Swedish Social Democrats* (New Jersey: The Bedminster Press, 1973) p. 699.
3. E. g. Marquis Childs, *Sweden: The Middle Way* (Yale University Press, 1936); Frank Parkin, *Class Inequality and Political Order* (London: Macgibbon & Kee, 1971); Richard Scase, *Social Democracy in Capitalist Society* (London: Croom Helm, 1977).
4. Walter Korpi, *The Working Class in Welfare Capitalism* (London: Routledge & Kegan Paul, 1978) p.81.
5. Castles, op. cit., pp. 118–131.
6. Castles, op. cit., pp. 68–69, Tables 2.3 and 2.4.
7. R. Meidener, *Coordination and Solidarity: An Approach to Wage Policy* (Stockholm: LO, 1974) p.4.
8. David Owen, *A Future that will Work* (London: Viking, 1984) p. 8.
9. Quotations taken from *Basic Programme of Social Democratic Party of Germany*, English edition published by the SPD, Bonn.
10. Willy Brandt, *Godesberg nicht verspielen* (Bonn: Ebert Stiftung, 1979) p. 4.
11. Willy Brandt, *People and Politics* (London: Collins, 1978) p. 147.
12. Klaus Harpprecht, *Willy Brandt* (Bonn: Abelard-Schuman, 1972) p. 6.
13. H. Becker, *Auf dem Weg zur lernenden Gesellschaft* (Stuttgart, 1980) p. 6.
14. Willy Brandt, *People and Politics* op. cit., p. 234.
15. See Lisanne Radice, *Beatrice and Sidney Webb: Fabian Socialists* (London: Macmillan, 1984) pp. 9–10, and pp. 211–12.
16. Philip Williams, *Hugh Gaitskell* (London: Cape, 1979) pp. 569–72.
17. Harold Wilson, *The New Britain: Labour's Plan* (Harmondsworth: Penguin, 1964) pp. 9–10.
18. See Michael Stewart, *The Jekyll and Hyde Years* (London: Dent, 1977) pp. 102–105.
19. Michael Stewart in Wilfred Beckerman (ed.), *The Labour Government's Economic Record* (London: Duckworth, 1972) pp. 110–11.
20. Castles, op. cit., p. 88.
21. See Castles, op. cit., pp. 61–4; Anthony Crosland *Socialism Now* (London: Cape, 1974) pp. 20–1; and W. Schwark and A. Wolf, 'West Germany', pp. 272–5 in *Educational Policy: An International Survey* (London: Croom Helm, 1984).
22. See Castles, op. cit., pp. 93–9.

2 The Climate Changes

1. E.g. C. P. Kindleberger, *Europe's Postwar Growth* (Harvard University Press, 1967); N. Kaldor, *Causes of the Slow Rate of Economic Growth of the United Kingdom* (Cambridge University Press, 1966); A. Maddison *Economic Growth in the West* (London: Allen & Unwin, 1964).
2. Andrea Boltho, 'Growth', pp. 16–20 in A. Boltho (ed.), *The European Economy: Growth and Crisis* (Oxford University Press, 1982).
3. Boltho, op. cit., pp. 18–19.
4. See the writings of Milton Friedman and F. A. Hayek.
5. See Andrew Shonfield, *The Use of Public Power* (Oxford University Press, 1982) pp. 34–6.
6. *Towards Full Employment and Price Stability* (Paris: OECD, 1977) p. 103.
7. John Llewellyn, *Lessons from Two Oil Shocks* (Paris: OECD Working Paper, 1983) p. 5.
8. Michael Stewart, *Controlling the Economic Future* (London: Wheatsheaf Books, 1983) pp. 61–2; Shonfield, op. cit., p. 74.
9. Quoted in Shonfield, op. cit., p. 45.
10. Stewart, op. cit., pp. 68–9.
11. Shonfield, op. cit., p. 79.
12. Llewellyn, op. cit., p. 10.
13. Llewellyn, op. cit., pp. 14–15.

3 The SPD

1. Speech at conference on Immanuel Kant, 12 March 1981.
2. See relevant OECD reports on West Germany.
3. 1977 OECD report.
4. Karl Kaiser, 'Schmidt's Foreign Policy', *New York Times*, 21 January 1979.
5. Jonathan Carr, *Helmut Schmidt: Helmsman of Germany* (Weidenfeld and Nicolson, 1985) p. 150.
6. See *The Financial Times*, 7 October 1980.
7. Carr, op. cit., pp. 165–70.
8. See relevant OECD reports.

4 The French Socialists

1. Denis MacShane, *François Mitterrand* (London: Quartet Books, 1982) p. 150.
2. Neill Nugent and David Lowe, *The Left in France* (London: Macmillan, 1982) pp. 57–8.
3. 1974 and 1975 OECD reports on France.
4. 1981 OECD report.
5. M. Sawyer, 'Income Distribution in OECD Countries' in *OECD Economic Outlook*, 1976.
6. R. W. Johnson, *The Long March of the French Left* (London: Macmillan, 1981) pp. 123–4.

7. Nugent and Lowe, op. cit., p. 246.
8. See Douglas E. Ashford, 'Decentralizing France' in J. S. Ambler (ed.), *The French Socialist Experiment* (Philadelphia: Institute for the Study of Human Issues, 1985).
9. 1983 OECD report.
10. 1984 OECD report.

5 The British Labour Party

1. Stewart, op. cit., p. 63.
2. 1979 *Public Expenditure White Paper*, Cmnd 7439.
3. Stewart, op. cit., p. 67.
4. Joel Barnett, *Inside the Treasury*, (London: Deutsch, 1982) pp. 104–10. Susan Crosland, *Tony Crosland* (London: Cape, 1982) pp. 381–2.
5. Stewart, op. cit., p. 68.
6. Giles Radice, 'The Significance of the British General Election', *Government and Opposition*, Summer 1979, pp. 276–281.
7. Peter Riddell, *The Thatcher Government* (Oxford: Martin Robertson, 1983), pp. 73–4.
8. William Keegan, *Mrs Thatcher's Economic Experiment* (London: Allen Lane, 1984) pp. 33–104.
9. Riddell, op. cit., p. 91.
10. See Ian Bradley, *Breaking the Mould* (Oxford: Martin Robertson, 1981) on the birth of the SDP.
11. David Butler and Dennis Kavanagh, *The British General Election of 1983* (London: Macmillan, 1984), pp. 296–7.
12. Butler and Kavanagh, op. cit., pp. 274–83.
13. See *The Economist*, 25 May 1985.

6 The Spanish Socialists

1. Jose Maria Maravall, *The Transition to Democracy in Spain* (New York: St. Martin's Press, 1982) pp. 140–1.
2. Santiago Carrillo, *Eurocommunism and the State* (London: Lawrence & Wishart, 1977).
3. Maravall, op. cit., pp. 150–1.
4. Robert Graham, *Spain: Change of a Nation* (London: Michael Joseph, 1984) p. 150.
5. Maravall, op. cit., pp. 173–7.
6. 1978 OECD report on Spain.
7. Graham, op. cit., pp. 270–1; Maravall, op. cit., p. 153.
8. Maravall, op. cit., pp. 154–9.
9. Elizabeth Nash, 'The Spanish Socialist Party since Franco', pp. 40–50 in D. Bell (ed.) *Democratic Politics in Spain* (London: Frances Pinter, 1983).
10. 1982 OECD report.
11. Bruce Young, 'The 1982 Elections', p. 140 in D. Bell (ed.), op. cit.
12. Maravall, op. cit., p. 195.
13. Maravall, op. cit., p. 208.

14. 1984 OECD report.
15. *Financial Times Survey*, 18 January 1985.
16. Robert Graham, *Financial Times Survey*, op. cit.

7 The Swedish Social Democrats

1. *Towards Equality*, The Alva Myrdal Report (Stockholm: Prisma, 1971).
2. *Towards Equality* op. cit., p. 13.
3. Rudolf Meidner, *Employee Investment Funds* (London: Allen & Unwin, 1978) p. 15.
4. 1975 OECD report.
5. 1976 OECD report.
6. Peter Walters, 'Sweden's Public Sector Crisis', *Government and Opposition*, Winter 1983, p. 27.
7. 1983 OECD report.
8. *The Swedish Budget 1983/84* (Stockholm: Ministry of Finance, 1983) p. 14.
9. *The Swedish Budget 1983/84* op. cit., p. 15.
10. 1985 OECD report and *The Swedish Budget 1985/86* (Stockholm: Ministry of Finance, 1985).

8 The Austrian Socialists

1. Melanie Sully, *Political Parties and Election in Austria* (London: Hurst, 1981) pp. 51–60.
2. Sully, op. cit., pp. 20–2.
3. Sully, op. cit., pp. 61–2.
4. Background paper prepared by Dr Hans Seidel for *American Enterprise Institute*, October 1981.
5. *Guardian*, 8 May 1979.
6. 1983 OECD report on Austria.
7. Edward März and Maria Szecsi, 'Austria's Economic Development 1945-1978', p. 128 in *Modern Austria* (Society for the Promotions of Science Scholarship, 1981).
8. Ferdinand Lacina, 'Development and Problems of Austrian Industry', p. 166 in K. Steiner (ed.), op. cit.
9. See Maria Szecsi, 'Social Partnership in Austria in K. Steiner (ed.), op. cit.
10. 1982 OECD report, p. 47.

9 Economic Policies

1. 1980 OECD report on West Germany.
2. Carr, op. cit., p. 99.
3. See relevant OECD reports on Austria.
4. E.g. *The Economist Survey*, 15 March 1980.
5. 1974 *London Business School Economic Outlook*.

6. Peter Hall, 'Socialism in One Country', p. 84 in P. G. Cerny and M. A. Schain (eds), *Socialism, the State and Public Policy* (London: Frances Pinter, 1985).
7. Hall, op. cit., p. 86.
8. 1984 OECD report on Spain.
9. 1984 OECD report on Spain, p. 7.
10. 1983 OECD report on Sweden.
11. Lacina, op. cit.
12. Based on House of Commons Library Research Division background paper.

10 Social Policies

1. David Heald, *Public Expenditure* (Oxford: Martin Robertson, 1983) pp. 38–41.
2, See Ramesh Mishra, *The Welfare State in Crisis* (London: Wheatsheaf, 1984) chapter 2.
3. Speech on 23 January 1976.
4. *Social Expenditure 1960–1990* (Paris: OECD, 1985) table 1.
5. Shonfield, op. cit. p. 31.
6. *Social Expenditure 1960–1990*, op. cit., table 3.
7. Barnett, op. cit., p. 32.
8. Nicholas Bosanquet, 'Labour and Public Expenditure', p. 39 in *Labour and Equality* (London: Fabian Society 1980).
9. Gerry Freeman, 'Socialism and Social Security', p. 107 in J. S. Ambler (ed.), op. cit.
10. *Social Expenditure 1960 1990*, op. cit., table 1.
11. *Guardian*, 9 October 1984.
12. Peter Walters, 'Distributing Decline', *Government and Opposition*, Summer 1985, p. 357.
13. Rudolf Strasser, *Social Policy since 1945*, p. 308 in K. Steiner, op. cit.
14. See *The New Programme of the SPÖe* (Vienna: SPÖe, 1978) p. 12.
15. Graham, op. cit., p. 126.
16. Mishra, op. cit., pp. 111–12.
17. Carr, op. cit., pp. 102–3.

11 Foreign Policies

1. Robert Putnam and Nicholas Bayne, *Hanging Together: The Seven Power Summits* (London: Heinemann, 1984) p. vii.
2. Denis Healey, *Labour and a World Society* (London: Fabian Society, 1985) p. 3.
3. Interview in *The Economist*, 6 October 1979.
4. Quoted by Roger Morgan, 'Dimensions of West German Foreign Policy, p. 74 in W. Patterson and G. Smith (eds), *The West German Model* (Cass, 1981).
5. Carr, op. cit., p. 124.
6. Carr, op. cit., p. 188.

7. Putnam and Bayne, op. cit., p. 97.
8. Carr, op. cit., p. 188.
9. Speech by James Callaghan, September 1975.
10. Putnam and Bayne, op. cit., p. 84-5.
11. Putnam and Bayne, op. cit., p. 85.
12. Jolyon Howarth, 'Defence Policy under Mitterrand', p. 112 in Cerny and Schain (eds), op. cit.
13. Putnam and Bayne, op. cit., p. 154.
14. Putnam and Bayne, op. cit., p. 185.
15. Peter Holmes, 'Spain and the EEC', pp. 169-75 in D. Bell (ed.), op. cit.
16. Graham, op. cit., p. 281.
17. *Financial Times Survey*, 18 January 1985.
18. Peter Jankowitsch, *Foreign Policy*, p. 378 in K. Steiner (ed.), op. cit.

12 Democratic Socialism

1. OECD *Economic Outlook* (Paris: OECD, June 1985) table 16.
2. OECD *Economic Outlook* (Paris: OECD, June 1979).
3. Christopher Huhne, *Guardian*, 28 November 1985.
4. See Bo Särlvik and Ivor Crewe, *Decade of dealignment* (Cambridge University Press, 1983).

Select Bibliography

This book is largely based on interviews and discussions. However, we have found the OECD reports on the economies of individual countries extremely useful; we have also consulted a number of newspapers including the *Financial Times, Le Monde, El Pais,* the *Guardian, The Times, The Economist.* The following works were also valuable:

AMBLER, J. S., (ed.), *The French Socialist Experiment* (Philadelphia: Institute for Study of Human Issues, 1985).

BARNETT, J., *Inside the Treasury* (London: Deutsch, 1982).

BELL, D. (ed.), *Democratic Politics in Spain* (London: Frances Pinter, 1983).

BOLTHO, A. (ed.), *The European Economy: Growth & Crisis* (Oxford University Press, 1982).

BRANDT, W., *People and Politics* (London: Collins, 1978).

CARR, J., *Helmut Schmidt: Helmsman of Germany* (London: Weidenfeld & Nicolson, 1985

CARR, R. and J. P. FUSI, *Spain: Dictatorship to Democracy* (London: Allen & Unwin, 1979).

CASTLES, F., *The Social Democratic Image of Society* (London: Routledge & Kegan Paul, 1978).

CERNY, P. G. and M. A. SCHAIN (eds), *Socialism, the State and Public Policy in France* (London: Frances Pinter, 1985).

CHILDS, M., *Sweden: The Middle Way on Trial* (Yale University Press, 1980).

CODDING, G.A. and W. SAFRAN, *Ideology and Politics: The Socialist Party of France* (Boulden Col.: Westview, 1978).

DAHRENDORF, R., *Society and Democracy in Germany* (London: Weidenfeld & Nicolson, 1960).

FELD, W. (ed.), *The Foreign Policies of West European Socialist Parties* (New York: Praeger, 1978).

FREARS, J.R., *France in the Giscard Presidency* (London: Allen & Unwin, 1981).

GRAHAM, R., *Spain: Change of a Nation* (London: Michael Joseph, 1984).

HANREIDER, W.F. (ed.), *West German Foreign Policy 1949–79* (Boulder, Col.: Westview, 1980).

HOUGH, J. R. (ed.), *Educational Policy: An International Survey* (London: Croom Helm, 1984).

JOHNSON, R.W., *The Long March of the French Left* (London: Macmillan, 1981).

KAVANAGH, D. (ed.), *The Politics of the Labour Party* (London: Allen & Unwin, 1982).

KEAGAN, W., *Mrs Thatcher's Economic Experiment* (London: Allen & Unwin, 1984).

KOLINSKY, M. and W. PATERSON (eds), *Social and Political Movements in Western Europe* (London: Croom Helm, 1976).

KORPI, W., *The Working Class in Welfare Capitalism* (London: Routledge & Kegan Paul, 1978).

MACSHANE, D., *Francois Mitterrand* (London: Quartet, 1982).

MARAVALL, J. M., *The Transition to Democracy in Spain* (London: Croom Helm, 1982).

MEIDNER, R., *Employee Investment Funds* (London: Allen & Unwin, 1978).

MENDERSHAUSEN, H., *Coping with the Oil Crisis: French and German Experiences* (Baltimore: Johns Hopkins University Press, 1976).

MERLINI, C. (ed.), *Economic Summits and Western Decision-Making* (London: Croom Helm, 1984).

MISHRA, R., *The Welfare State in Crisis* (London: Wheatsheaf, 1984).

MITTERRAND, F., *Ici et Maintenant* (Paris: Fayard, 1980).

MYRDAL, A., *Towards Equality* (Stockholm: Prisma, 1971).

NUGENT, N. and D. LOWE, *The Left in France* (London: Macmillan, 1982).

PARTI SOCIALISTE, *Projet Socialiste Pour La France des Annees 80* (Paris: Club Socialiste du Livre, 1981).

PATERSON, W. and A. THOMAS (eds), *Social Democratic Parties in Western Europe* (London: Croom Helm, 1977).

PUTNAM, R. and N. BAYNE, *Hanging Together: The Seven-Power Summitts* (London: Heinemann, 1984).

REYHER, L. , M. KOLLER and E. SPITZNAGEL, *Employment Policy Alternatives to Unemployment in the Federal Republic of Germany* (London: Anglo-German Foundation, 1980).

RIDDELL, P., *The Thatcher Government* (Oxford: Martin Robertson, 1983).

SHONFIELD, A., *The Use of Public Power* (Oxford University Press, 1985).

SERFATY, S. (ed.), *The Foreign Policies of the French Left* (Boulder, Col.: Westview, 1979).

STEINER, K. (ed.), *Modern Austria* (Alo Palto: Society for Promotion of Science and Scholarship, 1981).

STEWART, M., *The Jekyll and Hyde Years: Politics and Economic Policy since 1964* (London: Dent, 1977).

STEWART, M., *Controlling the Economic Future* (London: Wheatsheaf, 1984).

SULLY, M., *Political Parties and Elections in Austria* (London: Hurst, 1986).

TILFORD, R. (ed.), *The Ostpolitik and Political Change in Germany* (Farnborough, Hants: Saxon House, 1975).

WHITEHEAD, P., *The Writing on the Wall: Britain in the Seventies* (London: Michael Joseph, 1985).

WRIGHT, V., *The Government and Politics of France* (London: Hutchinson, 1978).

Index